Trump Tweets, The World Reacts

Trump Tweets, The World Reacts

Understanding What Is Relevant and Why

Edited by
Regina Luttrell

LEXINGTON BOOKS
Lanham • Boulder • New York • London

Published by Lexington Books
The Rowman & Littlefield Publishing Group, Inc.
4501 Forbes Boulevard, Suite 200, Lanham, Maryland 20706
www.rowman.com

Unit A, Whitacre Mews, 26-34 Stannary Street, London SE11 4AB

British Library Cataloguing in Publication Information Available

Library of Congress Cataloging-in-Publication Data

Library of Congress Control Number: 2018936926

ISBN: 978-1-4985-6308-6 (cloth)
ISBN: 978-1-4985-6309-3 (electronic)

™ The paper used in this publication meets the minimum requirements of American National Standard for Information Sciences—Permanence of Paper for Printed Library Materials, ANSI/NISO Z39.48-1992.

Printed in the United States of America

Contents

Acknowledgments

I would like to begin by first acknowledging the contributions of the professors that authored chapters in this volume. Without your original research, time, and expertise this book would still be just an idea. Thank you for trusting me and being a part of what has become a solid contribution to the literature.

My gratitude to Nicolette Amstutz and Lexington Books for supporting the book and seeing its value within the larger academic community.

Last, but never least, to those that matter most, Todd, Emma, and Avery, for your support.

Introduction

America Under a Trump Administration

Vicissitudes in Communication

Regina Luttrell

When the act of sending a tweet can destroy reputations, propel a company into turmoil, or move economic markets, it is not simply a tweet anymore. President Donald Trump's social habits have prompted an evolution within the communication landscape among journalists, politicians, government officials, and businesses alike. During his campaign, and well into his presidency, the president has used Twitter to communicate his reactions toward a multitude of topics. With this sentiment in mind, the following points are put forth for consideration.

After President Trump tweeted "Toyota Motor said will build a new plant in Baja, Mexico, to build Corolla cars for U.S. NO WAY! Build plant in U.S. or pay big border tax." Toyota's U.S.-traded shares fell almost 1 percent, lowering $2 billion from Toyota's total market value.[1] A similar tweet targeting Lockheed Martin stated "Based on the tremendous cost and cost overruns of the Lockheed Martin F-35, I have asked Boeing to price-out a comparable F-18 Super Hornet!" resulting in the company's shares falling approximately 2 percent, while shares of Boeing were up 0.5 percent. This tweet cut Lockheed Martin's market value by nearly $1.2 billion.[2] Even private citizens, including eighteen-year-old Lauren Batchelder, are not immune to becoming a target of Trump's Twitter lashings. The president tweeted "The arrogant young woman who questioned me in such a nasty fashion at No Labels yesterday was a Jeb staffer! HOW CAN HE BEAT RUSSIA & CHINA?" The following morning Batchelder's Facebook account, email, and voicemail were filled with threatening, often sexually overt, messages from angry Trump supporters condemning her for her actions.[3] Batchelder fled into hiding as her story was featured in main stream media and across social media outlets. In an analogous story, *New York Times* journalist, Serge F. Kovalesk, who suffers from arthrogryposis, was mocked at a Trump rally for his disability, Trump supporters cheered and jeered.[4] The president's opinions on the media have also been widely documented, including his assertion of CNN's "fake news," the *New York Times* "failing," and Buzzfeed "garbage"—all the while launching a full-throttle attack on the integrity of journalism. Respected journalist, Dan Rather, came out of retirement to launch "News and Guts," which promotes his vision of real journalism, news of integrity, and, as he would say, a "play no favorites, pull no punches" brand of reporting.[5] In these turbulent times, the public seeks nothing more than the truth. To further complicate matters, Kellyanne Conway, a trusted advisor to President Trump, introduced the notion of "alternative facts," prompting the Public Relations Society of America to issue a statement condemning "alternative facts" as unethical.[6] President Trump has even gone so far as to tweet "Just heard Foreign Minister of North Korea speak at U.N. If he echoes thoughts of Little Rocket Man, they won't be around much longer!" in response to the North Korean leader, Kim Jong Un, and his continued development of nuclear weapons.[7] The president has also used Twitter to publicly criticize the British prime minister, Theresa May, when he retweeted anti-Muslim videos from a far-right British political group.[8] "Theresa @thersa_may, don't focus on me, focus on the destructive Radical Islamic Terrorism that is taking place within the United Kingdom. We are doing just fine!"

As researchers we must ask ourselves what implications these interactions have, both within the United States and on the international stage. An insightful examination into the relevancy and importance of communication on social topics is one of the underlying premises of the book. The following chapters aim to illustrate and articulate the intimate connection between theories presented in communication and the mediums through which President Trump communicates. Drawing on a range of theoretical and empirical perspectives, this collection examines several transformations and implications of President Trump's influence on the social sphere, within economies, and the communications profession.

This text is appropriate to be utilized as a reference for both educators and social scientists who teach in the areas of public relations, journalism, social media, and mass communication. Graduate and undergraduate students will also find that many topics included in the book provide a foundation to better understand the implications of the social habits of arguably one the most influential men in modern society.

Individual chapters focus on four core areas—journalism, government, social media, and business. The objective of each chapter is to provide insight on the impact of the new "Tweeter-in-Chief" and consequences for public communications professionals and educators.

CHAPTER SYNOPSIS

Part I: Journalism

Chapter 1. Undiplomatic Diplomacy: The Challenges of Public Diplomacy in the Age of Trump
Stephanie Madden, Leysan Khakimova Storie, and Michael J. Steudeman

This chapter examines how Russian and U.S. newspapers covered the first 100 days of the Trump administration. The authors use a qualitative approach to study how the media framed Trump's executive actions and the public diplomacy implications based on these decisions. In addition to providing insights into how media in different countries covered the first 100 days of this administration, the answers to these questions may suggest important implications for public diplomacy via media relations.

Chapter 2. The News Media Framing of Trump: An Enigma or a Political Renegade
Arvind Diddi

Examines the news media framing of President Donald Trump before, during, and post presidential campaign. Scholarly studies have emphasized that the mainstream news media frames have public policy implications. Therefore, this chapter helps readers to understand not only what news was being covered about Trump, but also how that news was reported. Ultimately the chapter will reveal an understanding of the evolution of the present political atmosphere that led to the election of an unconventional president.

Chapter 3. "A Statement from the President": The Social Construction of News and Journalists' Use of Donald Trump's Tweets
Brian Moritz

This chapter explores the theory that if news is created by the routines, practices, and values of journalists, then to understand those is to understand the news itself. This chapter is a study of why President Donald Trump's tweets are viewed as newsworthy through the lens of the social construction of news, which is a key concept in the study of news and journalism.

Part II: Government

Chapter 4. China Is Laughing at Us. SAD! Trump's Twitter Diplomacy
Chiaoning Su and Paige L. Gibson

Based on content analysis and in-depth textual analysis, this chapter examines Trump's tweets on Taiwan and the subsequent coverage in six newspapers: *New York Times*, *Washington Post*, *Los Angeles Times*, *Boston Globe*, *Wall Street Journal*, and *Breitbart News*. Chapter 4 looks at Trump's social media habits and how they shape an international reality and its potential for foreign policy formation. Based on a content analysis of Trump's 433 tweets on China, the authors first investigate a variety of topical, rhetorical, and structural constructions used by Trump to conjure a specific image of China for his followers.

Chapter 5. Why Tweeting Makes for Bad Policy: President's Trump's Twitter Campaign and Its Shortchanging of Critical Thinking
Dwight DeWerth-Pallmeyer

The impact of our nation's ever-growing appetite for bite-sized messages delivered via "smart" phones has the impact of "dumbing down" both interpersonal communication, and typically works to poison a national conversation that would enhance our ability to work together. Tweeting from our commander-in-chief often leads to a continued pattern of antagonistic remarks that simply inflame raw emotion. A world of "tweets" works in opposition to pluralistic dialogue and critical thinking that could result in genuine solutions. The aim of this chapter is to examine President Trump's tweets during his first 100 days in office and demonstrate the nature of those tweets when pitted against Blooom's traditional taxonomy of critical thinking. The chapter also seeks to address the nature of those tweets: do they clearly outline policy objectives, or do they serve mainly as attacks against individuals and work to silence the varied perspectives that are inherently "democratic" in nature?

Part III: Social Media

Chapter 6. Presidential Twitter Storms: When Is President Trump Creating a Storm?
Jennifer Grygiel and Regina Luttrell

This chapter focuses on a specific form of presidential social media communications, called the "Twitter storm" and examines the manner in which President Donald Trump facilitates communication via Twitter, and the reactions from traditional media, who are often targeted by such Twitter storms. An analysis on the frequency of postinauguration tweets sent between February 1, 2017 and July 17, 2017 from the preexisting U.S. presidential Twitter handle @POTUS and the president's personal account, @realDonaldTrump was completed utilizing the social media data analytics program, Sysomos. The sentiments and tone of the tweets were also analyzed to gain a better understanding whether the administration was using one handle to communicate differently from the other.

Chapter 7. Total Losers, Highly Overrated: Donald Trump and Internet Trolling in Real Life
Robert J. Baron

This chapter contends that Donald Trump has effectively leveraged trolling as an ongoing social media and political strategy. The chapter explores three central areas: the general practice of internet trolling, tweets from the @realDonaldTrump account to see how Donald Trump has applied trolling practices to his own use of Twitter, and what Donald Trump's use of trolling, as one of the loudest voices on Twitter, means for this social media platform, and for our work as social media scholars and professionals.

Part IV: Business

Chapter 8. Trump, Trucks, and Twitter: The Auto Industry Case and Presidential Speech on Social Media
Steve A. Stuglin

Business executives have long looked to presidential speech for cues on policy that might impact a given industry. The auto industry, which has a complicated history with government and the presidency, is especially responsive to signals from Washington DC. Yet Donald Trump has demonstrated a willingness to engage directly with companies and individuals on Twitter in an unprecedented manner, complicating the relationship between the presidency and industry further. Chapter 8 inspects a series of exchanges between Donald Trump and domestic automakers in December 2016 and January 2017.

NOTES

1. James F. Peltz. "*Seattle Times*," seattletimes.com, https://www.seattletimes.com/business/wall-street-firms-use-algorithms-that-capture-trumps-tweets-to-profit-from-automated-trades/.
2. Christine Wang. "Lockheed Martin Shares Take Another Tumble after Trump Tweet," cnbc.com. https://www.cnbc.com/2016/12/22/lockheed-martin-shares-take-another-tumble-after-trump-tweet.html.

3. Jenna Johnson. “This Is What Happens When Donald Trump Attacks a Private Citizen on Twitter,” smh.com.au. http://www.smh.com.au/world/this-is-what-happens-when-donald-trump-attacks-a-private-citizen-on-twitter-20161209-gt86qb.html.

4. Glenn Kessler. “Donald Trump’s revisionist history of mocking a disabled reporter,” guides.mtholyoke.edu. http://guides.mtholyoke.edu/trump/news-media.

5. Library Research Guides, Mount Holyoke, “Trump Presidency: Election, Transition, and Administration,” guides.mtholyoke.edu. http://guides.mtholyoke.edu/trump/news-media.

6. Jane Dvorak. “PRSA Statement on ‘Alternative Facts,’” Public Relations Society of America. May 31, 2017, https://www.prsa.org/prsa-statement-alternative-facts/.

7. Associated Press, “Donald Trump Goes after Kim Jong Un on Twitter,” *Time*, November 30, 2017, http://time.com/5042837/donald-trump-north-korea-twitter-china/.

8. Akela Lacey. “Trump pushes back on May: ‘Don’t focus on me,’” politico.com, https://www.politico.com/story/2017/11/29/trump-theresa-may-muslims-270495.

Part I

JOURNALISM

Chapter One

Undiplomatic Diplomacy

The Challenges of Public Diplomacy in the Age of Trump

Stephanie Madden, Leysan Khakimova Storie, and Michael J. Steudeman

The first 100 days of President Donald J. Trump's foreign policy were described as a "whirlwind of activity, controversy, and chaos."[1] Exerting "America first" unilateralism, a hardline posture, and an unclear foreign policy doctrine, Trump followed through on campaign promises to break with decades of previous American public diplomacy. For just one notable example, Secretary of State Rex Tillerson ordered his department to reverse a decades-long commitment to promoting democracy abroad.[2]

The Trump administration's break with tradition creates much uncertainty. In the international arena, public diplomacy is historically one of the primary tools a nation has to communicate its values and foster understanding among nations. Diplomacy also encompasses the ways governments communicate with international audiences through forms of "soft power" including the arts, cultural exchanges, education programs, and new media engagement. Given its many forms, a dramatic change in tactics for public diplomacy may have lasting implications for the reputation of the United States and its relationship with other nations.

Framing theory helps explain the role of media coverage in shaping how publics, both international and domestic, interpret public diplomacy. Using a qualitative approach to framing, this study examines how media framed Trump's executive actions and the public diplomacy implications of those decisions. Because Trump's relationship with Russia has received a great deal of media attention, this study explored how both U.S. and Russian newspapers covered the first 100 days of the Trump administration. This approach provided insights into how media in different countries covered Trump's foreign policy, providing important implications for the conduct of public diplomacy via media relations. We begin with a review of relevant literature.

LITERATURE REVIEW

This literature review begins by exploring the historical role and implications of the U.S. president in foreign diplomacy. It then highlights how media plays an important role in shaping international public opinion. Finally, framing theory is reviewed and its effect on public diplomacy is considered.

The U.S. Presidency and Foreign Policy

Due to constitutional authority, institutional advantages, and limited public knowledge of foreign affairs, presidents have traditionally exerted far more autonomy in foreign than in domestic policy. The U.S. Constitution explicitly grants the president power as commander in chief. Likewise, it allows the president, with Senate consent, to make treaties and appoint foreign ambassadors.[3] Historically, from the Louisiana Purchase under Thomas Jefferson to the conduct of drone strikes under Barack Obama, presidents have regularly asserted this constitutional authority. Presidents have also had greater success garnering congressional support for their foreign, compared to their domestic, legislative priorities.[4]

In the twentieth century, major changes in communication heightened the president's authority over foreign policy. According to political scientist Jeffrey Tulis, the administrations of Theodore Roosevelt and Woodrow Wilson signaled a transition to a "rhetorical presidency." This transition heralded an expanded authority for shaping the "active and continuous presidential leadership of popular opinion."[5] Concurrently, presidents have also increasingly expanded their ability to act without public or congressional consultation through the consolidation of executive branch authority.[6] The confluence of these two shifts gives presidents unique power to modulate public opinion to shape their foreign policy decisions.[7]

Further compounding presidential authority, the public and media generally attend to foreign policy issues far less than domestic ones. In part, this is because foreign policy issues are more numerous and distant than domestic ones in voters' day-to-day lives.[8] More importantly, a great deal of trust is placed in the president for having superior knowledge of foreign events. Especially since the passage of the National Security Act of 1947, the president has held "near-monopoly control over information and expertise in foreign policy."[9] With direct oversight of agencies like the National Security Council and Central Intelligence Agency, presidents often enjoy congressional deference in military interventions. International agreements like the North Atlantic Treaty Organization further expand the president's diplomatic insight into foreign affairs.[10]

Owing to their expanded authority and greater likelihood for success, presidents tend to be particularly active in foreign policy. In a comprehensive overview of shifting political party ideologies between 1900 and 2009, Verlan Lewis argues that "parties in long-term control of the presidency tend to become more interventionist on foreign policy while parties in opposition tend to become less interventionist."[11] Beyond direct intervention, presidents also can exert long-term influence over the shape of foreign policy discourse. For instance, Mary Stuckey contends that President Jimmy Carter's rhetoric of human rights "helped make the issue a persistent theme in debates over US foreign policy."[12] Presidents enjoy the ability to frame such issues, tether them to national values, and educate the public about their importance.[13]

Given the outsized role of the president in foreign policy, international relations pose both opportunity and peril to incoming administrations in their first 100 days. During this period, presidents typically enjoy higher approval ratings, less press scrutiny, and greater congressional support than during other periods.[14] However, as former White House foreign policy advisors Kurt M. Campbell and James Steinberg write, these periods of transition are also fraught with difficulty. Compared to other nations, in the United States transitions are "prolonged and complicated affairs with thousands of people moving into new positions of responsibility."[15] During this period, presidents commonly face conflicting advice, leaks from disgruntled advisors, anxieties about getting "tested" by foreign adversaries, and the need to fill a large number of empty high-level positions in government.[16] In the aftermath of infamous early-presidency foreign policy disasters like the 1961 Bay of Pigs invasion, presidents have gradually developed a strong concern for managing foreign diplomacy, both tactically and communicatively.[17]

Public Diplomacy and Mass Media

Public diplomacy—government or organizational efforts to engage with foreign publics for a political purpose—has traditionally relied on mass media. Governments use various media to communicate with foreign publics, including radio, television, and print media.[18] Therefore, mediated public diplomacy can be defined as governments' attempts to control the framing of its policies in foreign media.[19]

Previous studies have suggested that media, including newspapers, play an important role in the formation of public opinion internationally. For example, Wanta, Golan, and Lee found that the more a foreign nation was covered in the media, the more likely U.S. citizens regarded that nation as important to the United States.[20] Negative coverage of a foreign country was associated with negative thinking about that country. Likewise, a later study found that the more positive coverage a foreign country received in the U.S. media, the more favorably that country viewed the U.S. public.[21] For those audiences that lack direct and personal experience with another nation, mass media is especially important in shaping their opinions about that nation.

Newspapers can be a useful tool in mediated public diplomacy. For example, the Chinese government used U.S. local newspapers to promote the visit of its president to the United States in 1997.[22] More recently, China used newspapers as one of the mediums to communicate with publics in West Africa and build a public diplomatic network.[23] However, the interplay of national and international politics may complicate the role of newspapers in public diplomacy. One example of this complexity occurred in Denmark in 2005. Despite an Islamic prohibition on publishing images of the Prophet Muhammad, a Danish newspaper published such illustrations. Several Muslim organizations and representatives of Arab countries in Denmark raised concerns about the images to the Danish government. The matter then escalated internationally, with Muslim publics and the Egyptian government criticizing Danish institutions for neglecting the situation. Research by Lindholm and Olsson suggested that the issue became a public diplomacy crisis due to Danish government's initial framing of the issue as a domestic issue, and its neglect of international stakeholders.[24]

Public Diplomacy, Power, and Legitimacy

The concept of public diplomacy and power are inextricably linked. The very concept of public diplomacy is often discussed in view of Joseph S. Nye's distinction between soft and hard power.[25] Hard power is government's effort to influence publics through coercion (i.e., military action or one-way communication), whereas soft power rests on attraction and "ability to shape the preferences of others."[26] Nye argued that soft power will be the essential element of international politics and the main force of public diplomacy in the twenty-first century.[27]

Another concept linked to soft power is legitimacy and credibility. Nations must have the moral authority to be able to reach foreign audiences.[28] One way to establish credibility is through consistency between words and behavior. For example, U.S. legitimacy was undermined by its dualist approach to the Middle East, in that the government argued for human rights and against terrorism, and yet it supported unjust treatment of Palestinians. Gass and Seiter argued that in order to exercise influence, governments must project not only power, but also credibility.[29] The authors suggest three dimensions of credibility: expertise, trustworthiness, and goodwill. Gass and Seiter also suggest that credibility is culture-bound and dynamic.[30] In other words, building credibility requires long-term effort and sensitivity. Both soft and hard power are desired in the political arena because they allow nations to pursue their goals.

Defining Framing Theory

Media often do not view international audiences as their target public, despite globalization and increased international connectivity.[31] Framing theory provides insight into how the media cover public diplomacy, which in turn influences how audiences make meaning of foreign policy and action. Frames are the "central process by which government officials and journalists exercise political influence over each other and over the public."[32] Frames have four primary functions: (1) define problems; (2) diagnose causes; (3) make moral judgments; and (4) suggest remedies.[33] Despite the general lack of media focus on international audiences, frames that employ more culturally resonant terms have more potential for influence.[34]

Frame Contests and Agenda Setting

Media power and independent framing have grown in coverage of foreign policy.[35] Media framing can range from total dominance by one frame to an evenly divided standoff between competing frames.[36] There is also a contest of frames coming from government sources versus the media frames about public diplomacy efforts. Historically, journalists tended to adopt frames provided by the government, particularly under the unifying framework of the Cold War paradigm.[37] Therefore, it was not uncommon to find overwhelmingly dominant frames in the coverage of foreign policy news. However, after the Cold War ended, journalists exercised greater autonomy in how news stories were framed.[38] For example, instead of White House–sanctioned frames dominating coverage of the Clinton administration's 1999 intervention in Kosovo with NATO, the media "tilted decisively *against* the administration."[39] In this case, the media composed and activated a counterframe that overwhelmed the official White House framing of the intervention.

Even with greater media freedom in foreign policy framing in the post-Cold War era, "outcomes can differ when a president employs culture, power, strategy, and motivations to convincingly portray a significant threat to the United States."[40] The Bush administration effectively did this in the aftermath of 9/11 by reviving deference to patriotism, lessening elite dissent, and dominating the media narrative with the clear threat of terrorism.[41] After 9/11, journalists used the War on Terror and Axis of Evil frames because they "felt obliged to follow the administration's framing," in part because dissenting with these frames could appear unpatriotic and counter to stopping the global threat of terrorism.[42] For presidential legacies and foreign policy, "statesmanship is less important than constructing villains and turning up the rhetorical heat on enemy states."[43]

While framing countries with positive or negative attributes has clear foreign policy implications, domestic issues such as immigration, also relate to foreign policy.[44] Throughout American history, immigration policy framing has "focused on the desirability or undesirability of letting in particular groups of people."[45] Media frames play an important role in shaping attitudes toward immigrants and ultimately defining the boundaries of national identity.[46] Arguments against immigration are generally framed as economic and public safety threats, whereas pro-immigration frames tend to focus on civil and human rights.[47] Jennifer Merolla and Elizabeth Zechmeister found that when terrorism is salient, people have increasingly negative attitudes toward immigrants.[48] This has implications for which countries are seen as harboring terrorists and anti-American sentiment, and the rhetorical stance that the president will take toward both the leadership and citizens of foreign nations.

Based on this literature review, the follow research questions guided this study:

RQ1: How did the U.S. media frame the first 100 days of the Trump administration?

RQ2: How did the Russian media frame the first 100 days of the Trump administration?

METHODS

This study used a qualitative content analysis to explore how U.S. and Russian media framed the first 100 days of the Trump administration and the potential public policy implications. This method is appropriate for small sample sizes and exploratory research.[49] The study focused on the framing in the United States and Russia because of the Trump administration's highly publicized connections with Russia and its leadership.

The study's total sample consisted of two hundred articles in Russian and U.S. national newspapers. The sample was limited to articles appearing in the newspapers between January 20 and April 29, 2017, which constituted Trump's first 100 days in office. The Russian sample consisted of one hundred articles from five national daily newspapers with the widest circulation and included *Izvestia*, *Komsomol'skaia Pravda*, *Moskovskii Komsomolets*,

Rossiiskaya Gazeta, and *Kommersant*. One of the researchers for this project is a native Russian speaker. The five national newspapers selected for the U.S. sample based on circulation were *USA Today,* the *New York Times,* the *Wall Street Journal,* the *Los Angeles Times,* and the *New York Post.*

The search term used for both the U.S. and Russian sample was simply "Trump." This phrase was purposefully selected to avoid a sample limited by specific countries or by academic phrases like "public diplomacy." Unsurprisingly, this yielded thousands of results for each of the top five U.S. newspapers searched. To limit the sample to make it possible for qualitative content analysis, one hundred articles were randomly selected from each newspaper by using a random number generator. Therefore, the original U.S. sample consisted of one hundred articles from five newspapers such as the *New York Times* and the *Washington Post*. Then, the researcher read through the articles and selected the first twenty articles from each paper with relevance to Trump and foreign policy issues. Several articles were eliminated because the stories did not directly relate to Trump's public diplomacy actions or perceptions. The same process was followed to create a sample of Russian articles.

The U.S. articles were gathered using LexisNexis Academic and Factiva databases. The Russian articles were gathered using the Universal Database of Russian Newspapers.

The five highest circulating newspapers in 2016 in the United States and Russia were chosen for the U.S. sample. The articles were collected online in July and August 2017. To analyze the data we used a deductive approach that involved data reduction, data display, conclusion drawing, and verification.[50]

As part of the data reduction process we developed a preliminary coding sheet based on the research questions and prior literature on framing, public diplomacy, and the U.S. presidency.

Throughout this iterative process, these codes were refined, collapsed, and added as necessary. In the data display phase researchers used an Excel spreadsheet that included the research questions, codes, and examples for each code.

In the conclusion drawing and verification phase, the researchers discussed the results in the spreadsheet. In answering the research questions, we compared the data from the Russian and U.S. newspapers, building a chain of evidence. Conclusion drawing and verification occurred throughout the analysis process.

RESULTS

RQ1: How did the U.S. media frame the first 100 days of the Trump administration?

Four themes emerged from the coverage of the Trump administration in the first 100 days from the U.S. newspaper sample. These were *internal conflict, questionable ethics*, *instability and uncertainty*, and a *break from tradition.*

Internal Conflict

A predominant focus across news outlets in the first month of the Trump presidency was on the conflict within the United States surrounding "Trump's public embrace of a 'Muslim ban'" as a national policy decision with major foreign policy implications.[51] Articles focused on the human interest stories of those impacted by this ban, activist efforts to protest the policy, and the autonomy local governments have to overrule the decision and remain sanctuary cities. Coverage of those affected by the decision discussed those "whose lives were upended by the executive order" and were "shaken and deeply worried about what comes next."[52] There were activist protests at many airports throughout the nation, with the *LA Times* reporting that the scene was "both frantic and somber at LAX."[53] In addition to opposition from other political leaders, U.S. media reported that business leaders decided "it's a bigger risk to their investors and bottom line to stay quiet than it is to protest Trump's ban on refugees and travel from seven Muslim-majority nations."[54]

In addition to citizen opposition to the ban, media framed legal opposition through courts as a source of internal conflict. For example, the *Wall Street Journal* reported that "travel restrictions on six majority-Muslim nations, intended to diminish terrorism threats, are mired in the courts."[55] Trump's reaction to the legal opposition manifested in the firing of then Acting Attorney General Sally Yates.[56]

Internal conflict also manifested with local level politicians, who did not like the infringement on historical autonomy in decisions about being sanctuary cities to be superseded by a federal travel ban framed as an anti-terrorism initiative. The mayor of New York City is quoted in the *New York Post* as saying "President Trump issued an executive order today and its purported purpose was to enhance public safety. But here in New York City, and in cities across this nation, this executive order could, in fact, undermine public safety and make our neighborhoods less safe."[57]

Questionable Ethics

Newspapers discussed three prominent ethical issues pertaining to the Trump administration in the first 100 days: (1) the influence of Trump's business dealings on his presidency; (2) the involvement of the Trump team in Russian meddling in the 2016 election; and (3) the president's former national security adviser Michael Flynn's connection to Russia. Discussion of Trump's business dealings and the impact this would have on his presidency focused primarily on foreign relations with China. Specially, coverage discussed the "condemnation from U.S. ethics lawyers and Democratic lawmakers . . . who question whether the president violated the Constitution by accepting special favors from a foreign government."[58]

The Trump administration's connections to Russia, though, prompted the most frequent discussions of questionable ethics. Coverage ruminated on investigations into "whether Russia meddled in the 2016 election and if Team Trump was involved—as the president unloaded on Twitter, putting out his own spin and blasting Democrats."[59] In addition to the questions of whether Russia meddled in the election results, *USA Today* examined the resignation of national security Advisor Michael Flynn "over his failure to disclose phone conversations with the Russian ambassador about U.S. sanctions imposed on Moscow."[60] Likewise, the *Wall Street Journal* focused on Flynn "taking payments linked to foreign governments."[61] The *New York Times* reported that he had been "paid over $65,000 by companies linked to Russia in 2015."[62]

Instability and Uncertainty

Articles describe the first 100 days of Trump's presidency using words like "uncertainty," "anxiety," "geopolitical risk," and "diplomatic fracas." For example, the *LA Times* reported that "the manner in which the White House is introducing policy is sowing uncertainty and geopolitical risk that's worrying American businesses on the global market," adding that unease could grow "if the White House continues to shun norms and lash out at its biggest trading partners."[63] An article about an immigrant hub in the *LA Times* says, "On the street, talk of Trump is everywhere. It's mostly critical. And it's tinged with anxiety and uncertainty."[64]

The *Wall Street Journal* described Trump as the "mercurial new president" in an article about revising the executive order to remove Iraq from the travel ban.[65] In discussing the administration's personnel, the article said that the "national security team had been left out of deliberations."[66] They added that the instability of the Trump administration's first 100 days stemmed from Trump's arrival "with no governing experience, and in particular no military or foreign-affairs experience."[67] Furthermore, despite being critical of taking military action against Syria, he "reportedly changed his mind when confronted with graphic photos of Syrian children killed and wounded in the gas attack."[68] Because of the "confusion and chaos coming from the White House over its foreign policy," diplomats and U.N. officials are primarily turning to others, such as U.N. ambassador Nikki Haley, "for clarity on a wide range of policies from Syria to Iran, Israel and Russia."[69]

Break from Tradition

Much of Trump's policy strategy is discussed as a direct reversal of the Obama administration's policies. For example, the Trump administration is described as offering "sweeping reforms that reverse many of former president Barack Obama's immigration policies—and allow the United States to give the boot to virtually every illegal immigrant in the country."[70] While the specifics of the Trump administration's foreign policy were unclear, it was clear that hard power versus soft power would be a guiding principle. As the *LA Times* reported, "the Trump administration has indicated human rights will not be a public priority."[71] Another example can be found when "President Trump delivered an ultimatum to Chinese leader Xi Jinping in advance of their first presidential meeting this week at Mar-a-Lago: Contain North Korea's aggression or the United States will."[72] These examples frame the Trump presidency as preferring hard power and aggressive posturing toward countries with which the United States has previously tried to maintain positive relationships.

Although the Trump administration is not the first to have an antagonistic relationship with the media, Trump's level of "distrust and ridicule of the media is unlike anything they have seen from a commander in chief."[73] The usage of new media—in particular Twitter—to express this disdain with the media and "fake news" was also viewed as a break with past practices of presidential decorum. The *LA Times* reported that "Trump used Twitter—as he often does—to voice his disdain for questions about Russia."[74] This article then quotes one of Trump's tweets, which has become a primary source for presidential quotes in media coverage: "It is the same Fake News Media that said there is 'no path to victory for Trump' that is now pushing the phony Russia story. A total scam!"[75]

RQ2: How did the Russian media frame the first 100 days of the Trump administration?

Four themes emerged from the coverage of the Trump administration in the first 100 days from the Russian newspaper sample. These were *hope with a grain of salt*, a *president under pressure, hard power and America first*, and *sources of information.*

Hope with a Grain of Salt

Articles published in the end of January and in February framed Trump's presidency as a positive *change* and even a *revolution*. An article in *Izvestiia* portrayed Trump starting his presidency with "action on all fronts," including foreign policy, national policy, social issues, and even changes in the White House building.[76] Stories covered Trump's decision to remove the LGBT section from the White House, to change the immigration policy, to "shake the American elite," and overall "to rebuild America."[77]

The first two months of Trump's presidency were discussed with a lot of hope for collaboration between Russia and the United States The *international collaboration* frame was one of the most frequent frames and mostly related to Trump's efforts to build a good relationship with Russia. For example, the lead to the article published in *Izvestia* on February 7 stated, "It seems that Russia and the United States are entering the phase of closer economic and political ties."[78] Another article in *Kommersant*, published on February 1, discussed the first telephone call between the Russian and U.S. presidents and their determination to work together.[79] The international collaboration frame appeared rarely in articles from March and April 2017.

At the same time, Russian newspapers sought to curb enthusiasm about Trump's presidency, especially in articles published in March and April 2017. One article published on April 12 had a headline "The end of a romance that has not started."[80] Luk'ianov of *Rossiiskaia Gazeta* wrote on April 12 that the relationship between Russia and the United States was returning to "normal—mutual rejection and confrontation."[81] Some articles called for patience, suggesting that changes take time and that Trump would need at least a year to make the necessary appointments and start restoring relationships with Russia.

President under Pressure

Trump was portrayed as an active leader and a good citizen, but also a president who had conflicts with other branches of U.S. government and media. Articles with the *political strength* frame reported about Trump as an active president. For example, *Izvestiia* reported that "Donald Trump achieved more during his first two weeks than his predecessors, even though they faced much better conditions."[82] Other articles praised Trump's "bravery" for speaking the "truth" about global warming and discussed his decision to attack Syria as a sign of a strong president.[83] He was portrayed as a good citizen, who paid his taxes and declined to receive a salary during his presidency.[84] However, articles published in late March and April signaled a weakening image of Trump. An article published on March 21 had a headline "Americans got disappointed with Trump," discussing low approval ratings in the United States.[85] Other articles also suggested that Trump was not strong enough to change his country's relationship with Russia. Trump's limitations in engaging with the world, especially Russia, were explained in light of internal U.S. politics, blaming the other actors for blocking Trump in bringing the expected changes.[86]

Internal Conflict/Competition

This frame was the most frequent frame, portraying Trump as having many conflicts with other branches in the U.S. government. For example, a headline in *Izvestia* read, "Trump declared a war on the Washington establishment."[87] Another article in Moskovskiy Komsomolets stated, "Russia cannot ignore Trump's objective domestic political problems and cannot but notice that the new U.S. president's freedom is considerably restricted when dealing with our country."[88] Trump's adversaries were described as liberals, Democrats, "russophobes" who were against working with the Russian government, and who were planning Trump's impeachment. The *legitimacy* frame relayed concerns about president's ability to lead the country, Democrats' efforts to impeach Trump, his age, and his mental ability.[89]

The other weaknesses in Trump's presidency included his struggles to build a cabinet. The *personnel* frame related to Trump's struggles to make necessary appointments, his inability to retain appointed officials, and his decision to appoint family members to White House roles.[90] Already in February, an article suggested that Trump's press secretary, Sean Spicer, was likely to lose his job.[91] Several articles discussed Michael Flynn losing his position as a national security advisor, suggesting that it was a mistake and a sign of weakness for Trump to let him go.[92]

Foreign Policy Intertwined with Internal Conflict

Russian newspapers associated Trump's presidency with *hard power,* a frequent frame in the sample. The *soft power* frame appeared only once. Articles discussed Trump's efforts to make the U.S. military the best in the world, his plans to increase the military budget, and his interest in developing nuclear power.[93] Newspapers also discussed the attack in Syria as viewed positively by other actors within the United States, including the U.S. media that had been previously critical of him. The attack on Syria was discussed as a symbol of Trump-style foreign diplomacy, stressing Trump's limited consultation with internal and international actors, informing them rather than consulting with them.[94]

The *international conflict/competition* frame relayed the tensions between Trump and other governments as well as international organizations, including NATO, North Korea, and some world leaders. For example, articles on Trump's meeting with Germany's chancellor, Angela Merkel, discussed the disagreements between the two leaders. The conflict between the U.S. government and Russia, including the issue of sanctions imposed by the U.S. government on Russia, was discussed widely. Regarding the claims about Russia's interference in the U.S. elections, one newspaper article stated that "Kremlin denies any involvement in the U.S. political processes and views the [court] hearings as a U.S. internal issue."[95] Newspapers described some members of congress and senate as russophobes, blamed President Obama for imposing the sanctions, and framed Trump as unable to resolve that conflict. For example, one article in *Kommersant* had a headline "Donald Trump is not allowed access to sanctions."[96] In other words, articles distinguished between the U.S. president and the other government entities such as the Senate and the Congress, as well as the previous U.S. president. Moreover, articles suggested that the Russia-U.S. conflict was used as a justification for increasing military spending. For example, an article in *Moskovskii Komsomolets* stated:

> Conversations about "aggressive Russian aspirations" always intensify whenever the federal budgeting is approaching, and now is exactly the time in the United States. A strong enemy is needed to justify the growing military spendings, which are increasing solely in the interest of the large-scale defense businesses. Russia fits the role [of the enemy] very well.[97]

The articles discussed a new shift in global powers following Trump's election. The *economic consequences* frame covered the reduced funding of international organizations, the shrinking of the State Department budget, and the increase in the U.S. military spending. Articles discussed the impact of Trump's presidency on the U.S. economy, suggesting that his isolationist approach weakened the United States and the global economy.[98] Several articles reflected on the role that Russia would play in that new political and economic system. For example, in an article titled "Trump dumped China," reporter Inna Degot'kova discussed Trump's decision to withdraw from the Trans-Pacific Partnership, stating it signaled the United States' "renunciation of the global trade leadership role." The article further noted that the "USA forces Russia to rethink about its role and place in international trade due to the emergence of new global settings."[99]

Sources of Information

Articles in Russian newspapers discussed the issue of truth in Trump's time, doubting the authenticity of information coming from the U.S. media and the internet. For example, one article questioned the authenticity of videos from Syria that put the Russian and Syrian army in a negative light.[100] Another article doubted the credibility of the U.S. media related to the reporting about the relationship between Michael Flynn and the Russian government. Russian newspapers discussed American media reports as lacking evidence and sometimes offensive (i.e., when U.S. reporter Bill O'Reilly asked Donald Trump about Putin, calling the Russian president "a killer").[101]

Trump's dissatisfaction with the media and the nature of reporting was evident due to his claims about "fake news," "lies," and his overall conflict with "liberal media."[102] Several articles discussed leaks to the media, Trump's investigation into the leaks, and his claims that President Obama was behind those leaks.[103] Russian newspapers also mocked U.S. media for their lack of objectivity.[104] Despite the criticism of U.S. media, Russian newspapers often relied on U.S. newspapers and television for information, and quotes from major newspapers such as the *Washington Post*, the *New York Times* and the *Wall Street Journal* appeared in the articles. Television news channels were also used as a source and included NBC News, Fox News, and MSNBC. Often articles referred to social media, including Donald Trump's Twitter account, Facebook posts by Russian prime minister Dmitri Medvedev, and social media statements by Russian senators.

DISCUSSION

There was a lack of a dominant frame from the first 100 days of the Trump presidency in both the U.S. and Russian newspaper samples. For the U.S. newspapers, this is not surprising given the greater autonomy journalists have experienced in framing international news since the Cold War.[105] However, the questions of truth and legitimacy, and the Trump administration's antagonistic relationship with the news media may have led to this greater fragmentation of framing. It is also difficult to frame or even articulate a president's policy when so much of the discussion around the president is his legitimacy to be president, founded on Russian election interference and lack of governing experience. One clear focus of the Trump administration in the first 100 days was to undo previous actions of the Obama administration. In Russian media, the "legitimacy of the president" frame was not only applied to Trump, but also used to question the legitimacy of the Obama administration. So, Trump's actions were seen as a direct reaction to "illegimate actions" of the Obama administration, indirectly giving legitimacy to Trump's actions even if there was not a clear strategy behind them besides undoing Obama-era policies.

The messages coming from the Trump administration rely on a media strategy that harkens back to the Bush administration in the aftermath of 9/11, based on rooting out terrorism and protecting American safety.[106] However, the U.S. newspapers analyzed in this study are combatting this with counter-frames to those that the administration is providing. Rather than "evil" and "threat" of radical Islam, many stories focus on the human interest of immigrants who live in the United States, those trapped and detained at the airport, and the irreparable damage policies like the "Muslim ban" have on the United States' international reputation.

In a quote that is apropos to describing Trump's presidency, Entman wrote that "presidents who crave political recognition and glory can draw this lesson: statesmanship is less important than constructing villains and turning up the rhetorical heat on enemy states."[107] We not only see Trump doing this toward enemy states such as North Korea, but more broadly his statesmanship is about constructing everyone who does not agree with him as the villain, including the news media, the opposition party, local level politicians, and even the nation's judicial system. Interestingly, though, while past American presidents have framed Russia as an enemy state and villain, the Trump administration's numerous ties to Russia has changed this approach. The implications of this change in strategy can be seen in the Russian newspaper articles framing Trump as a positive revolutionary change and as a person willing to collaborate with Russia.

Russian media were more optimistic at the beginning of the Trump presidency, however, optimism decreased toward the end of the first 100 days of his tenure in the White House, with the internal conflicts of national policy seen as a barrier to Trump's international engagement. The analysis of Russian papers reflected a nuanced portrayal of the American political system. Interestingly, Russian newspapers separated the U.S. president from the Senate and Congress as well as the judicial system, which allowed them to communicate a positive image of Trump but negatively cover the American political system. Both U.S. and Russian newspapers comment on the limited role that policy experts and advisors play in Trump's decisions. In the U.S. sample, focus was placed on foreign policy veteran Nikki Haley as someone that people were turning to in order to understand the strategy behind the president's actions. The Russian media placed more attention to the key advisor roles that Trump's family had in the administration.

The role of new media in influencing and shaping international relations and foreign diplomacy decisions is a major contribution of this study. In the U.S. and Russian articles analyzed for this study, oftentimes the official quotes and messages from the Trump administration were taken from the president's tweets. This 140-character presidency may be leading to many the impressions of the Trump administration as being unstable, uncertain, and mercurial. Twitter lacks nuance, therefore, developing a foreign policy strategy is difficult. Instead, reactionary and hard power posturing is coming through, which Russian media was viewing as political strength and decisiveness. American media, on the other hand, used this to further question the legitimacy of the president and draw attention to a lack of governing experience.

CONCLUSION

Negative coverage of uncertainty and turmoil in American politics may be seen as an opportunity for Russia. The first 100 days of the Trump administration present a unique case in public diplomacy where a president is covered negatively in their own country, but positively in a different country. It becomes even more complex when these two countries have been historical adversaries. Interestingly, though, Russian newspapers relied heavily on American media to report about Trump. Despite the overall negative tone of the U.S. media, Russian media turned around this negative coverage and framed it positively.

NOTES

1. Hal Brands, "6 Things We Know about Trump's Foreign Policy after 100 Days," *Foreign Policy*, April 26, 2017, http://foreignpolicy.com/2017/04/26/6-things-we-know-about-trumps-foreign-policy-after-100-days/.

2. Josh Rogin, "State Department Considers Scrubbing Democracy Promotion from Its Mission," *Washington Post*, August 1, 2017, https://www.washingtonpost.com/news/josh-rogin/wp/2017/08/01/state-department-considers-scrubbing-democracy-promotion-from-its-mission/?utm_term=.6fe84a9b8021.

3. U.S. Const. art. 2, § 2.

4. Brandice Canes-Wrone, William G. Howell, and David E. Lewis, "Toward a Broader Understanding of Presidential Power: A Reevaluation of the Two Presidencies Thesis," *The Journal of Politics* 70 (2008): 1–16.

5. Jeffrey K. Tulis, *The Rhetorical Presidency* (Princeton, NJ: Princeton University Press, 1987), 17–18.

6. Vanessa B. Beasley, "The Rhetorical Presidency Meets the Unitary Executive," *Rhetoric & Public Affairs* 13 (2010): 7–35.

7. Matthew A. Baum, "Going Private: Public Opinion, Presidential Rhetoric, and the *Domestic* Politics of Audience Costs in U.S. Foreign Policy Crises," *Journal of Conflict Resolution* 48 (2004): 611.

8. Baum, "Going Private," 610.

9. Robin F. Marra, Charles W. Ostrom, Jr., and Dennis M. Simon, "Foreign Policy and Presidential Popularity: Creating Windows of Opportunity in the Perpetual Election," *Journal of Conflict Resolution* 34 (1990): 591.

10. Ibid.

11. Verlan Lewis, "The President and the Parties' Ideologies: Party Ideas about Foreign Policy since 1900," *Presidential Studies Quarterly* 47 (2017): 28.

12. Mary Stuckey, "Jimmy Carter, Human Rights, and the Instrumental Effects of Presidential Rhetoric," in *The Handbook of Rhetoric and Public Address*, ed. Shawn J. Parry-Giles and J. Michael Hogan (East Lansing: Michigan State University Press, 2009), 294.

13. Ibid., 299.

14. Matthew N. Beckmann and Joseph Godfrey, "The Policy Opportunities in Presidential Honeymoons," *Political Research Quarterly* 60 (2007): 250–251.

15. Campbell, Kurt M. and James Steinberg, *Difficult Transitions: Foreign Policy Troubles at the Outset of Presidential Power* (Washington, DC: Brookings Institution Press, 2008), 2.

16. Ibid., 2–3.

17. Ibid., 90; 111.

18. For example, Mohammed El-Nawawy, "U.S. Public Diplomacy in the Arab World: The News Credibility of Radio Sawa and Television Alhurra," *Global Media and Communication* 2 (2006): 183–203; Julia Ioffe, "What is Russia Today?" *Columbia Journalist Review* 49 (2010): 44–49; Guy Golan and Evhenia Viatchaninova, "The Advertorial as a Tool of Mediated Public Diplomacy," *International Journal of Communication* 8 (2014): 1268–1288; Philip Seib, "Transnational Journalism, Public Diplomacy, and Virtual States," *Journalism Studies* 11 (2010): 734–744; Annabelle Sreberny, Marie Gillespie, and Gerd Baumann, "Epilogue: The BBC World Service and the Middle East—Past, Present, and Future Dilemmas," *Middle Eastern Journal of Culture and Communication* 3 (2010): 279–285; Jian Wang and Tsan-Kuo Chang, "Strategic Public Diplomacy and Local Press: How a High-Profile 'Head of State' Visit was Covered in America's Heartland," *Public Relations Review* 30 (2004): 11–24.

19. Robert M. Entman, "Theorizing Mediated Public Diplomacy: The U.S. Case," *Press/Politics* 13 (2008): 87–112.

20. Wayne Wanta, Guy Golan, and Cheolhan Lee, "Agenda Setting and International News: Media Influence on Public Perception of Foreign Nations," *Journalism & Mass Communication Quarterly* 81 (2004): 364–377.

21. Suman Lee and Hyehyun Hong, "International Public Relations' Influence on Media Coverage and Public Perceptions of Foreign Countries," *Public Relations Review* 38 (2012): 491–493.

22. Wang and Chang, "Strategic Public Diplomacy."

23. Di Wu and Aimei Yang, "China's Public Diplomatic Networks on the Ebola Issue in West Africa: Issues Management in a Network Society," *Public Relations Review* 43 (2017): 345–357.

24. Kristina Lindholm and Eva-Karin Olsson, "Crisis Communication as a Multilevel Game: The Muhammad Cartoons from a Crisis Diplomacy Perspective," *International Journal of Press/Politics* 16 (2011): 254–271.

25. Joseph S. Nye, *Soft Power: The Means to Success in World Politics* (New York: Public Affairs, 2004).

26. Ibid., 5.

27. Ibid.

28. Shibley Telhami, *The Stakes: America in the Middle East* (Boulder, CO: Westview Press, 2002).

29. Robert H. Gass and John S. Seiter, "Credibility and Public Diplomacy," in *Routledge Handbook of Public Diplomacy*, ed. Nancy Snow and Philip M. Taylor (New York, NY: Routledge, 2009), 154–165.

30. Ibid.

31. Leysan Khakimova Storie, Stephanie Lynne Madden, and Brooke Fisher Liu, "The Death of Bin Laden: How Russian and U.S. Media Frame Counterterrorism," *Public Relations Review* 40 (2014): 429–439.

32. Robert M. Entman, "Cascading Activation: Contesting the White House's Frame after 9/11," *Political Communication* 20 (2003): 417.

33. Lynn M. Zoch and Juan-Carlos Molleda, "Building a Theoretical Model of Media Relations Using Framing, Information Subsidies, and Agenda-Building," in *Public Relations Theory II*, ed. Carl H. Botan and Vince Hazleton (Mahwah: Lawrence Erlbaum Associates, 2006): 279–309.

34. Entman, "Cascading Activation."

35. Robert M. Entman, *Projections of Power: Framing News, Public Opinion, and U.S. Foreign Policy* (Chicago: University of Chicago Press, 2004).

36. Entman, "Cascading Activism."

37. Seth C. Lewis and Stephen D. Reese, "What Is the War on Terror? Framing through the Eyes of Journalists," *Journalism & Mass Media Quarterly* 86 (2009): 85–102; Entman, *Projections of Power.*

38. Entman, *Projections of Power*, 104.

39. Ibid., 98 (italics in original)

40. Ibid., 104.

41. Ibid.

42. Lewis and Reese, "What is the War on Terror," 791.

43. Entman, *Projections of Power,* 99.

44. Michael Teitelbaum, "Immigration, Refugees, and Foreign Policy," *International Organization* 38 (1984): 429–450.

45. Chris Haynes, Jennifer L. Merolla, and S. Karthick Ramakrishnan, *Framing Immigrants: News Coverage, Public Opinion, and Policy* (New York: Russell Sage Foundation, 2016), 4.

46. Stephanie A. Fryberg, Nicole M. Stephens, Rebecca Covarrubias, Hazel Rose Markus, Erin D. Carter, Giselle A. Laiduc, Ana J. Salido, "How the Media Frames the Immigration Debate: The Critical Role of Location and Politics," *Analyses of Social Issues and Public Policy* 12 (2012): 96–112.

47. Ibid.

48. Jennifer L. Merolla and Elizabeth J. Zechmeister, *Democracy at Risk: How Terrorist Threats Affect the Public* (Chicago: University of Chicago Press, 2009).

49. Sharlene Hesse-Biber and Patricia Leavy, *The Practice of Qualitative Research*, 2nd ed. (Thousand Oaks, CA: Sage Publishing, 2011).

50. Matthew B. Miles, A. Michael Huberman, and Johnny Saldana, *Qualitative Data Analysis: A Method Sourcebook* (Thousand Oaks, CA: Sage Publishing, 2013).

51. Cathleen Decker, "Trump Scores Few Wins So Far," *Los Angeles Times*, March 17, 2017, https://www.pressreader.com/usa/los-angeles-times/20170317/281724089364529.

52. Jennifer Medina, "He Was Sent Back to Iran. Now, a Court Says the U.S. Must Readmit Him," *New York Times*, January 30, 2017, https://www.nytimes.com/2017/01/30/us/iran-brothers-travel-ban-ali-vayeghan.html?mcubz=1.

53. James Queally, Alene Tchekmedyian, and Dakota Smith, "7 Detained at LAX in Trump Ban," *Los Angeles Times*, January 28, 2017, http://www.latimes.com/loca/lanow/la-me-ln-lax-immigration-vigil-20170128-story.html.

54. David Pierson, "Why Corporations Can't Risk Keeping Silent about Trump's Immigration Ban," *Los Angeles Times*, January 31, 2017, http://www.latimes.com/politics/washington/la-na-trailguide-updates-why-corporations-can-t-risk-keeping-1485876546-htmlstory.html.

55. Louise Radnofsky and Rebecca Ballhaus, "Donald Trump Racks up Few Wins so Far," *Wall Street Journal*, April 1, 2017, https://www.wsj.com/articles/donald-trump-racks-up-few-wins-so-far-1490997606.

56. Mark Moore, Marisa Schultz, Daniel Halper, and Bruce Golding, "Trump Stands Firm against Immigration Ban's Critics," *New York Post*, January 30, 2017, http://nypost.com/2017/01/30/trump-stands-firm-in-wake-of-massive-immigration-ban-backlash/.

57. Michael Gartland and Bob Fredericks, "Trump's 'Sanctuary City' Funding Threat Could Cost NYC $7B," *New York Post*, January 26, 2017, http://nypost.com/2017/01/26/trumps-sanctuary-city-funding-threat-could-cost-nyc-7b/.

58. Jessica Meyers, "The Day of Trump Toilets and Condoms in China May Have Just Ended," *Los Angeles Times*, March 6, 2017, http://www.latimes.com/world/asia/la-fg-china-trump-trademark-2017-story.html.

59. Marisa Schultz, Mark Moore, and Bob Fredericks, "Sending Don in a Spin," *New York Post*, March 21, 2017, https://www.pressreader.com/usa/new-york-post/20170321/281599535319860.

60. Oren Dorell, "Donald Trump's Ties to Russia Go Back 30 years," *USA Today*, February 15, 2017, https://www.usatoday.com/story/news/world/2017/02/15/donald-trumps-ties-russia-go-back-30-years/97949746/.

61. Byron Tau, "Pentagon Opens Probe into Michael Flynn's Foreign Payments," *Wall Street Journal,* April 27, 2017, https://www.wsj.com/articles/pentagon-opens-probe-into-michael-flynns-foreign-payments-1493303790.

62. Adam Goldman and Michael Schwirtz, "Document Sheds New Light on Flynn's Links to Russia," *New York Times*, March 16, 2017, https://www.nytimes.com/2017/03/16/us/politics/michael-flynn-russia-paid-trip.html.

63. Pierson, "Why Corporations Can't Risk Keeping Silent about Trump's Immigration Ban."

64. Ruben Vives, "'They're so Scared.' Trump Brings Heartache, Fear in L.A.'s 'Ellis Island,'" *Los Angeles Times*, March 24, 2017, http://www.latimes.com/local/lanow/la-me-trump-boyle-heights-20170321-htmlstory.html.

65. Tamer El-Ghobashy, Peter Nicholas, Felicia Schwartz, and Ben Kesling, "Why Trump, against His Instincts, Spared Iraq from the Travel Ban," *Wall Street Journal*, April 3, 2017, https://www.wsj.com/articles/why-trump-against-his-instincts-spared-iraq-from-the-travel-ban-1491231782.

66. Ibid.

67. Ibid.

68. Joe Tacopino and Chris Perez, "Trump Strikes," *New York Post*, April 7, 2017, https://www.pressreader.com/usa/new-york-post/20170407/281479276269888.

69. Farnaz Fassihi, “Nikki Haley’s Role at U.N. in the Spotlight,” *Wall Street Journal*, April 10, 2017, https://www.wsj.com/articles/nikki-haleys-role-at-u-n-in-the-spotlight-1491875492.

70. Marisa Schultz and Bob Fredericks, “NYC Refuses to Give Gang Members to I.C.E.,” *New York Post*, February 22, 2017, https://www.pressreader.com/usa/new-york-post/20170222/281487866118191.

71. Tracy Wilkinson and Noah Bierman, “Egypt’s Authoritarian-Minded President Gets a Warm White House Welcome,” *Los Angeles Times*, April 3, 2017, http://www.latimes.com/nation/la-fg-na-pol-trump-sisi-20170403-story.html.

72. Mark Moore and Marisa Schultz, “It’s Mao or Never,” *New York Post*, April 3, 2017, https://www.pressreader.com/usa/new-york-post/20170403/281672549789353.

73. Stephen Battaglio, “President Trump Will be a Boon and Challenge for the Cable News Business,” *Los Angeles Times*, January 20, 2017, http://www.latimes.com/business/hollywood/la-fi-ct-cnn-trump-20170116-story.html.

74. Kurtis Lee, “Most Americans Favor an Independent Inquiry into Trump Associates’ Ties with Russia, Poll Shows,” *Los Angeles Times*, April 1, 2017, http://www.latimes.com/politics/la-na-russia-poll-20170401-story.html.

75. Ibid.

76. Iurii Bogdanov, “Konservativnyi Renessans Donal’da Trampa,” *Izvestiia*, February 6, 2017, URL; Edvard Chesnokov, “Vmeste s Trampom s Oval’nyi kabinet v’ekhal Cherchill,” *Komsomol’skaia Pravda*, January 25, 2017.

77. Bogdanov, “Konservativnyi Renessans Donal’da Trampa”; Igor’ Dunaevskii, “Tramp Meniaet Poriadki,” *Rossiiskaia Gazeta*, January 31, 2017; Evgenii Chernykh, “Staryi Tramp Borozdy ne Isportit?” *Komsomol’skaia Pravda*, January 25, 2017; Igor’ Dunaevskii, “O Rossii–ni Slova,” *Rossiiskaia Gazeta*, March 2, 2017.

78. Aleksandr Pasechnik, “Novatsii ot Trampa,” *Izvestiia*, February 07, 2017.

79. Sergei Strokan’, “Donal’d Tramp Vybral Korolia,” *Kommersant Daily*, February 1, 2017.

80. Fedor Luk’ianov, “Konets ne Nachavshegosia Romana,” *Rossiiskaia Gazeta*, April 12, 2017.

81. Ibid.

82. Iurii Bogdanov, “Dve Nedeli Donal’da Trampa,” *Izvestiia*, February 3, 2017.

83. Vadim Ustinov, “Donal’d Tramp Ub’et Evropeiskii Avtoprom,” *Moskovskii Komsomolets*, February 9, 2017; Georgii Bovt, “Kak Tramp is Plokhogo Vmig Stal Khoroshim,” *Komsomol’skaya Pravda*, April 10, 2017.

84. Liubov’ Glazunova, “Taina Nalogov Trampa Raskryta,” *Moskovskii Komsomolets*, March 16, 2017; Renat Abdullin, “Tramp Obustroil Sebe Kabinet,” *Moskovkii Komsomolets*, February 10, 2017.

85. Liubov’ Glazunova, “Amerikantsy Razocharovalis’ v Trampe,” *Moskovskii Komsomolets*, March 21, 2017.

86. Kira Latukhina, “Pereshli Chertu,” *Rossiiskaia Gazeta*, April 10, 2017.

87. Aleksei Zabrodin, “Tramp Ob’iavil Voinu Vashingtonskoi Mashine,” *Izvestiia*, January 23, 2017.

88. Mikhail Rostovskii, “Tramp Nam Ne v Pomoshch’,” *Moskovskii Komsomolets*, February 9, 2017.

89. Aleksei Zabrodin, "'Kartochnyi Domik' Dlia Donal'da Trampa," *Izvestiia*, February 27, 2017; Evgenii Cherhnykh, "Staryi Tramp Borozdy ne Isportit?" *Komsomol'skaia Pravda*, January 25, 2017.

90. Aleksei Osipov, "Klan Trampa," *Komsomol'skaia Pravda*, January 24, 2017.

91. Evgenii Shestakov, "Tramp ustal chitat' lozh'," *Rossiiskaia Gazeta*, February 9, 2017.

92. Renat Abdullin, "Tramp Povtoriaet Oshibki Niksona," *Moskovskii Komsomolets*, March 3, 2017.

93. For example, Viktor Baranets, "Tramp-pam-pam I Nash Bol'shoi Babakh," *Komsomol'skaia Pravda*, March 1, 2017; Ol'ga Bozh'eva, "Tramp Otkopal Topor Voiny," *Moskovskii Komsomolets*, March 10, 2017.

94. Sergei Strokan', "Donal'd Tramp Stavit Ambitsioznye Misheni," *Kommersant*, April 10, 2017.

95. Renat Abdullin, "Kongressmeny Metiat v Trampa." *Moskovskii Komsomolets*, April 3, 2017.

96. Pavel Tarasenko, Elena Chernenko, Vladimir Dzaguto, Ol'ga Mordiushenko, and Iuliia Poliakova, "Donal'da Trampa ne Dopuskaiut do Sankstii," *Kommersant*, February 9, 2017, URL.

97. Ol'ga Bosh'eva, "Tramp Otkopal Topor Voiny," *Moskovskii Komsomolets*, March 10, 2017.

98. Vitalii Gaidaev, "Vlasti SShA Podderzhali zoloto." *Kommersant*, February 7, 2017.

99. Inna Degot'kova, "Tramp Kinul Aziu," *Moskovskii Komsomolets*, January 25, 2017.

100. For example, Vadim Poegli, "Tramp Molodets," *Moskovskii Komsomolets*, April 10, 2017, Kira Latukhina and Konstantin Volkov, "Pereshli Chertu," *Rossiiskaia Gazeta*, April 10, 2017.

101. Khovanskaia Asia and Abbas Dzhuma, "Donal'd Tramp: Iran Gosudarstvo-Terrorist Nomer Odin!" *Komosmol'akaia Pravda*, February 7, 2017.

102. Elena Chrnenko and Mikhail Korostikov, "Donal'd Tramp Pripechatal Pressu," *Kommersnant*, February 27, 2017; Edvard Chesnokov, "Tramp Ishchet Krota v Belom Dome," *Komsomol'skaia Pravda*, February 11, 2017; Evgenii Shestakov, "Tramp Ustal Chitat' Lozh'," *Rossiiskaia Gazeta*, February 9, 2017.

103. Aleksei Zabrodin, "Tramp Ishchet Podderzhki v Obshchestve Protiv Liberal'nykh SMI," *Izvestiia*, March 1, 2017; Georgii. Bovt, "Kak Tramp iz Plokhogo Vmig Stal Khoroshim," *Komsomol'skaia Pravda*, April 10, 2017.

104. Entman, *Projections of Power.*

105. Ibid.

106. Ibid., p. 99.

107. Entman, Robert M. *Projections of Power: Framing News, Public Opinion, and U.S. Foreign Policy*. Chicago: University of Chicago Press, 2004.

Chapter Two

The News Media Framing of Trump

An Enigma or a Political Renegade

Arvind Diddi

Democracy and journalism are the two sides of the same coin. For a governing process by the people, for the people, and of the people, such as democracy, free, vibrant, and robust news media are a must. The news media are supposed to serve as the healthy counterbalance to the democracy, however, the relationship between these two is seldom smooth. While history is rife with such tumultuous relationships between the news media and the democratic process, the 2016 presidential campaign took this usually rocky relationship to a new height. Indeed, the prevailing political atmosphere, the presidential candidates, and an overworked news media, added to the overall dynamics.[1] A charged and deeply divided American polity craved a radical change. The Republican candidate, Donald Trump, defied all political norms and made his bid for the highest office of the land straight from being an entrepreneur and reality show entertainer.[2] On the other hand, Trump's Democratic rival, Senator Hillary Clinton, despite being on the verge of creating a history as the first woman president of the United States, continued to court controversy over the emails from her tenure as the secretary of state and her inescapable links to the Clinton Foundation. And the news media found themselves overstretched in covering these two overexposed candidates, their controversies, and the bitter rivalry consuming the entire American electorate.[3]

This chapter, especially then, examines the news media framing of President Trump before, during, and post presidential campaign. Scholarly studies have emphasized that the news media frames have public policy implications.[4] Studying news media frames help understand not only what news was being covered about Trump, but also how that news about him was being covered. What aspects of Trump's candidacy, campaign, and presidency were being *selected* and made *salience* in the communicated messages[5] are the essence of his news media frames. What can be learned from these news media frames? How close were these frames to the truth that the news outlets are required to cover as per their professional ethics guidelines? In the process of discharging their constitutionally responsible duty, it has been made evident that not only the White House press corps, but also the news media, in general, are facing new and unprecedented challenges in covering the present administration.[6] It is important, however, to put this challenge being faced by the news media in a broader perspective by understanding the evolution of the present political environment that led to the election of an unconventional candidate as the president.[7] The question of whether the media created Trump was put in perspective by Mazzoleni[8] through filmmaker Michael Moore's quote, and then summing it up with his observation. He wrote, quoting Moore from his Facebook post, moments after Trump won the 2016 election, "Trump's victory is no surprise. He was never a joke. Treating him as one only strengthened him. He is both a creature and a creation of the media and the media will never own that."[9] Although media did not create Trump's persona, they did contribute to build up his political visage, albeit negative. "At the end the media may have been complicit in the defeat of Hillary Clinton, a candidate who was all but advantaged by a (too) favorable media frenzy," Mazzoleni[10] argued.

PROFESSIONAL CODE OF ETHICS FOR THE NEWS MEDIA

American founding fathers realized the importance of a free press to the democracy. Thus, they ensured the protection of free press under the First Amendment. Despite being fresh out of the armed Revolutionary War leading to the American freedom from the British rule, they had a clear understanding that the pen is mightier than the sword. Hence, it can be argued that the right to bear arms came as a part of the Second Amendment and not the First. Also, the word "press" was used as print was the only mass medium existing during that time. And this press freedom now can be applied to most media dealing with free and ethical news. In this backdrop, what professional code of conduct should guide the news media? For instance, the Society of Professional Journalists (SPJ) code of ethics prescribes these four tenets to journalists/news media professionals—"Seek truth and report it, minimize harm, act independently, and be accountable and transparent."[11] These guiding principles for journalists started taking a clearer shape toward the beginning of the twentieth century. Thus, the objectivity in news reporting is somewhat a concept of the last century. From the American Revolutionary War in late 1700 through the Progressive Era, coinciding with the Muckraking period in journalism, ending in the early 1900s, press objectivity didn't exist as it is understood and interpreted in the present day. The SPJ's code of ethics is clear and concise, and following it until the beginning of twenty-first century was manageable with the traditional news media. But, with the advent of the internet and fast-evolving social media, this digital era has put forth new challenges in front of the practice of ethical journalism as the lines among facts, opinions, analysis, interpretations, and rumors seem to be blurring, and giving rise to terms like "alternate facts." The news media, especially the online and the social media, are peppered with the phenomenon called the fake news. With the gatekeeping role of the traditional news media long gone and with the possibility of any-one getting on to the bandwagon of the news, the avenues for spreading fake news have increased, which if not addressed soon can pose grave threat to the democracy. Corporates like Google, Facebook, and Twitter have taken some initiatives to mitigate the instances of fake news on the social media. In this context, did the news media abide by their respective code of conduct while covering the 2016 presidential race? How did they cover Clinton and her campaign? How did they cover Trump, his campaign, and his administration? For instance, a Gallup Poll tracking from July 11 to September 8 found that Americans usually associated Clinton with words like "email, lie, health, speech, and foundation." In contrast, they associated Trump with words like "speech, president, immigration, Mexico, convention, campaign, and Obama."[12] What kind of challenges did the news media face in the ethical news coverage of Trump? How should the existing ethics guidelines be adapted to the evolving political challenges and rapid technical advances?

NEWS MEDIA FRAMING AND SPIRAL OF SILENCE

In mass communication research among various approaches the framing concept has been studied as a set of boundary conditions similar to framing of a painting or a photograph, and as a central organizing theme. Entman provided a comprehensive definition of framing, "To frame is to select some aspects of a perceived reality and make them more salient in a communicating text, in such a way as to promote a particular problem definition, causal interpretation, moral evaluation, and/or treatment recommendation for the item described."[13] In the context of this classic definition, how were news media perceiving and presenting Trump in their news coverage? What aspects about Trump were being selected and made salient? How was Trump being described? How was he being interpreted and morally evaluated for the audience? What solutions were being offered by the news media about Trump and his administration? And with regard to Trump's supporters, were they being subjected to a spiral of silence during the run up to the election day? In other words, did a sizeable number of these people decide to remain silent about being Trump supporters, fearing that if they openly express their preference even they will be stuck with labels such as bigot, misogynist, homophobic, and so on, exclusively reserved for Trump?

News Media Frames of Trump's Run Up to Candidacy

What was Trump as he announced his serious intention to run for the White House? Even after announcing his bid for the Republican Party nomination, how was he viewed and covered by the news media? These two questions are important to understand how the news media framed Trump in his initial bid and ascent to the political zenith. As a well-known New York businessman, often sought for his idiosyncrasies and unpredictability on the entertainment media scenario and reality shows like "The Apprentice," Trump was primarily framed as an *entertainment figure* capable of boosting the TRPs (target rating points).[14] This fact that Trump was good for TRPs during the 2016 presidential race is evident through this quote from the CBS chief executive officer Leslie Moonves: "It may not be good for America, but it's damn good for CBS."[15] The year leading to the primaries is also considered critical by the political scholars, and they term this period as "the invisible primary," wherein the candidates set the stage for a winning campaign with the help of media exposure that could play a make or break role.[16] From the time of the official announcement of his candidacy on July 16, 2015, to winning the major party nomination on July 19, 2016, the news media frames of Trump ranged from *he should be stopped* at any cost to *he is getting serious* about running for the highest office of the land. Despite facing opposition within the Republican Party and acerbic coverage in the news media, Trump's winning the nomination surprised everyone including political pundits and the seasoned Republican candidates like Ted Cruz, Marco Rubio, and Jeb Bush, to name a few.

News media and journalists go by what they know. They knew Trump for his outrageous statements and entertainment value, and they both sell. Going by the journalistic norms of the news values—Impact, Newness, and Proximity—Trump was high on his uniqueness, which relates to the *newness* news value. He was unique because he didn't have any political credentials unlike his immediate Republican rivals, but still surging in the nomination process based on his outspoken statements, unbridled use of social media, especially Twitter, and an exponentially surging fan base. Thus, during the initial phase of the primaries the news media continued to cover Trump as an *entertainment figure* in this backdrop of an unfolding "political reality show."[17] According to a study of the pre-primary news coverage by the Harvard Kennedy School's Shorenstein Center on Media, Politics and Public Policy:

> Although his [Trump's] incendiary remarks on immigrants and other issues brought him the biggest headlines, they were the smaller part of his coverage. Only 12 percent of Trump's coverage addressed his issue stands and political beliefs. Most of what was reported about Trump was in the context of the horserace and campaign activity, and was framed around his move to the top, a positive storyline that was uninterrupted except for a brief drop in the polls following remarks that he would require all Muslims in the United States to register with the federal government. Such coverage accounted for 56 percent of Trump's coverage and, of it, 79 percent was favorable in tone. News references to Trump's poll standing ran nine-to-one in his favor. Moreover, not everything that was said about Trump's personal characteristics and issue positions was negative in tone. Over 40 percent of it was positive in tone, often in the form of statements by voters who agreed with his policy positions or liked his personal style. A Washington Post piece, for example, quoted a Trump supporter as saying, "When Trump talks, it may not be presented in a pristine, PC way, but . . . [h]e's saying what needs to be said." Immigration was the issue that worked most clearly in Trump's favor. Although news coverage of his position included criticisms, it was accompanied by statements of solidarity from Republicans and was framed as the issue that was propelling him upward in the polls.[18]

As Trump embarked on his nomination journey on a victorious note, the news media played along by continuing to frame him as an *entertainment figure* high on braggadocio and outrageous comments. Trump's supporters liked what they saw and read about him in the news, despite negativity and lack of political correctness. To them, he provided simple answers as mentioned in the *Washington Post* article, "If you don't like immigration, build a wall. If you're suspicious of Muslims, track them in a database. If you support police officers, impose the death penalty on cop killers. These are thrilling ideas to many voters, especially when a candidate like Trump articulates them with such authority."[19] The news media used Trump primarily for boosting their business.[20] They assumed that he would run out of steam in the early stages of the primaries amid seasoned Republican candidates, and turn into his own nemesis, largely due to his abrasive rhetoric and lack of relevant political experience and political correctness.[21]

As Trump's steady rise in the political arena became increasingly clear and obvious to the news media the *uniqueness* news value quickly started morphing into the *impact* news value. The news media started getting into a damage control mode by shifting their focus to *he should be stopped frame* from the *entertainment figure frame*. Trump was only expected to provide a short-lived entertainment value to the serious business of politics and then disappear into oblivion. To the news media's chagrin this didn't happen. As articulated in a *Politico* article:

> Much of the Trump coverage has devoted itself to predicting his early political demise—not exactly the kind of press clips a candidate covets. In June [2015], when Trump announced [candidacy], the consensus press view was that he had no chance to win. As his campaign geared up in July and he climbed in polls, the press and the commentariat declared that peak Trump. (See *Washington Post* . . . NBC News . . . and Politico). But that turned out to be a false peak, as Trump continued to rise in August. This prompted additional stories about him peaking . . . *Weekly Standard* Editor William Kristol grew so certain Trump's end was near that he signed the candidate's death certificate on Twitter 10 times between July 20 and August 14.
>
> Somehow Trump's rise in the polls persisted, taking him higher and then higher still, clearing 30 percent in the Real Clear Politics average before the CNN debate. He lost that debate in a pitiable performance, said CNN, *Weekly Standard*, Vox, Real Clear Politics, Bloomberg Politics, the Daily Beast and others. The press promptly rearmed for another round of "peaked" stories . . . [*Politico*'s] Ben Schreckinger filed a piece analyzing the decline in Trump mentions on social media, TV, and radio, and his drop in the prediction markets to show Trump fever was finally breaking. In the New Yorker, Ryan Lizza wrote that a lack of a "second act" to Trump's campaign would spell his doom. "The beginning of the end of Donald Trump?" asked the headline in a new piece by the Washington Post's Dana Milbank. "Trump's Last Stand?" echoed the Atlantic headline. "The Beginning of Trump's End?" the Slate headline agreed.[22]

And in a way the news media started seeing the end of the honeymoon period in Trump's initial political coverage through the primaries, which had lasted longer than they had anticipated. This can also be tied to the journalistic norms. Once journalists commit to a certain metanarrative about a candidate and the campaign, then they find it hard to argue against it, and it is equally hard for them not to highlight trivial developments that foster the stereotypes.[23]

The news media tend to treat early primaries and caucuses as decisive events, with clear winners and losers. They started acknowledging Trump campaign juggernaut by framing it as *he is getting serious* and now it is hard to stop him from clinching the Republican Party nomination. According to the Shorenstein Center's study of the 2016 presidential primaries:

> With his three victories, Trump got most of the headlines, and the bulk of the coverage. Victory for Trump was also his path to positive coverage. During the primaries, journalists tend to build their narratives around the candidates' positions in the race. This focus leads them into four storylines: a candidate is "leading," "losing," "gaining ground," or "losing ground." Of the four storylines,

> the most predictably positive one is that of the "gaining ground" candidate. It's a story of growing momentum, rising poll numbers, ever larger crowds, and electoral success. The storyline invariably includes negative elements, typically around the tactics that the candidate is employing in the surge to the top. But the overall media portrayal of a "gaining ground" candidate is a positive one. That was the thrust of Trump's coverage in the opening contests of the 2016 campaign. The first line in The Washington Post's story out of South Carolina exclaimed, "Donald Trump commandingly won the South Carolina primary on Saturday night, solidifying his position as the front-runner for the Republican presidential nomination."
>
> Trump got positive press out of his electoral success. On the other hand, his issue stands and character were sources of negative press. By this point in the campaign, reporters had settled on their meta-narratives—the characterizations they were using in reporting on each of the candidates. In Trump's case, that narrative included the claim that he was strong and decisive. Those positive elements rested alongside more negative ones—that he was bigoted, insulting, unprepared, and narcissistic. As his victories piled up and it was clear that Trump had his opponents on the run, the horse race got less press attention, reducing the positive press stemming from his electoral success. News references to his policies and character, though still the smaller share of his coverage, were increasing in number and were largely negative in tone. Such claims were typically expressed, not by journalists directly, but through the words of political opponents and voters. Said a Wall Street Journal article: "Mr. Trump's cocky style has turned off some supporters, including Ralph Rife, a disabled coal miner in Slate Creek who voted for him but now says he can't stomach him. 'He's like a loose cannon,' Mr. Rife says."[24]

Having cemented his place as the Republication presidential candidate, Trump left no choice for the news media but to give him the coverage that the candidate's position commands in the American democratic system.

News Media Frames of Trump during the Presidential Campaign

With Trump in the driver's seat as one of the major party candidates, he had the news media continue to follow him in droves. But, what changed in the news coverage since his nomination confirmation and the presidential campaign's last lap from Labor Day to the day of election? The news media realized that they have been in some way complicit in giving Trump the edge to clinch the Republican Party nomination, and now it kind of dawned on them that he can be in the White House in a few months. The news media in a way wanted to undo what they did in the primaries by favoring Trump's coverage[25] and get a more politically qualified Clinton elected to the highest office.[26] According to a study of the news coverage of the 2016 general election, "His [Trump's] coverage was negative from the start, and never came close to entering positive territory. During his best weeks, the coverage ran two-to-one negative over positive. In his worst weeks, the ratio was more than ten-to-one. If there was a silver lining for Trump, it was that his two best weeks were the ones just preceding the November balloting."[27] The duel between Trump and the mainstream news media has become synonymous with the 2016 race. While Trump attacked the mainstream news media for being "biased" and trying to "rig" the election to favor Clinton,[28] the news media framed him as *unfit* to lead the nation and *dangerous*.[29] The news media framed Trump as *unfit* to lead the nation because of his lack of political experience and political correctness. He was framed as *dangerous* for his comments on women, Muslims, minorities, and immigration. As the 2016 general election study summed up:

> Trump's policy issues got less coverage during the general election than did a series of controversies that began with his attack on the Gold Star parents Khizr and Ghazala Khan after they had criticized him in a speech at the Democratic convention. That was followed by controversies involving the Trump Foundation, his refusal to release his tax returns, his avoidance of paying federal taxes, his allegation that the system was rigged against him, and his refusal ("unless I win") to say that he would accept the election outcome. Trump's most heavily covered controversy was triggered by the release of a video that captured him on microphone bragging about groping women without their consent, saying that "when you're a star, they let you do it." It was made public in early October, driving Trump's negative coverage from the 70-percent range into the 90-percent range.
>
> . . . He trailed Clinton in the polls at virtually every stage of the general election, which, in the press's horserace narrative, made him a "likely loser," which is a negative story. The other areas of Trump's coverage were even more negative. News reports focusing on his personal qualities were 82 percent negative to 18 percent positive. His policy stands were widely criticized—coverage in that area was 85 percent negative to 15 percent positive. His leadership qualities and experience were treated even more harshly—93 percent negative to 7 percent positive. The controversies enveloping his candidacy were also a source of bad news. Collectively, they ran 92 percent negative to 8 percent positive—a ratio of 11-to-1.[30]

The wordy duel between Trump and the mainstream media is lasting beyond the election, and is likely to be an unending saga surpassing his presidential tenure. During the election campaign, however, he topped his mainstream news media coverage through social media. In the study of the 2016 campaign, Patterson sums it up, "To journalists, the real issues of presidential politics are not the candidates' policy commitments but instead the controversies that ensnare them. The 2016 campaign fit the pattern to a tee. Everything from Clinton's emails to Trump's taxes was grist for the media mill. They accounted for 17 percent of the coverage—one in every six news reports."[31]

News Media Frames of Trump after Assuming the Office

On the expected lines, the Trump administration's coverage started on a rocky note picking up where the campaign coverage ended. A Pew Research Center (PRC) study on covering Trump during the early days of administration found that the news outlets, regardless of their political orientation, covered similar news agenda. They primarily framed their coverage of the Trump administration around character and leadership rather than policy.[32] Another PRC study,[33] while examining the Trump administration's first 100 days, found that his tweets became a source for the news outlets. During this period, stories with his tweets stood out from those that did not. The news coverage was more likely to have a negative assessment of the administration and also included challenges by the journalists to something the former said. During this time the news media focused their frames around *the president's leadership and character* and *his core ideology and policy agenda*. An example of *core ideology and policy agenda frame*, for instance, could be a news story about health care framed around the legislative differences in what the administration is proposing versus members of Congress. On the other hands, such a story with *selection* and *salience* around the evaluation of the president in terms of his outreach to and relationship with members of Congress would fall under the *leadership and character frame*.[34] The mainstream news media's focus on the new, unconventional president's administration was so stark that the voices of citizens got sidelined in the overall news coverage. According to a PRC's study on the initial coverage of Trump's presidency,[35] the low level of citizen voices were evident in the following five areas of news coverage—the president's political skills, immigration, appointments and nominations, U.S.-Russia relations, and health care. Across these five topics source attribution to everyday Americans never rose above 7 percent. The study on covering Trump in a polarized media environment further shed light on the news coverage of the present and previous three presidencies:

> Compared with the first 60 days of the Clinton, Bush and Obama presidencies, news outlets' evaluations of Trump's start in office were far more negative and less positive. About six-in-ten news stories about Trump's first 60 days (62%) carried an overall negative assessment of his words or actions. That is about three times more negative than for Obama (20%) and roughly twice that of Bush and Clinton (28% each).
>
> Coverage was also far less positive, with just 5% of stories conveying an overall positive assessment of the president and the administration. This is in

sharp contrast to Obama's first days in 2009, when 42% of the stories offered an overall positive assessment. While the difference is less pronounced, coverage of Bush's and Clinton's early days was still at least four times as positive as Trump's (22% and 27%, respectively).

. . . Another major difference between the coverage of Trump's first days in office and that of his last three predecessors is in the way journalists framed the coverage of the day's events—whether more around leadership and character or the policy agenda and ideology of the president and new administration. In previous years, the leadership and character frame never comprised more than half of overall coverage. In 2017, however, nearly seven-in-ten stories (69%) employed this lens. Coverage focusing on ideology and agenda, on the other hand, dropped from 50% in 2009 (a level lower than previous years) to about a third (31%) in 2017.[36]

The new, turbulent dynamic between the Trump administration and the mainstream news media has led to some symbolic and consequential changes in journalism.[37] News organizations like the *New York Times* and Reuters have sent guidelines to their journalists on professionally covering the president and his administration. For instance, Reuters guidelines stated that it is committed to ethical and impartial journalism with a focus on people, getting more resourceful with finding sources and worry less about official access, and never give in to intimidation.[38]

DISCUSSION

The political world and the mainstream journalism community were not prepared for the Trump presidency. As they are trying to understand the outcome of the 2016 presidential campaign and what the future holds under the new administration, a common question they have, is Trump an enigma or a political renegade? And the answer is, he is both. Enigma, because by no means he fits the description of a president in terms of his political experience and temperament, but he still managed to become the president. Trump is a political renegade because, as argued by Jonathan Rauch,[39] Trump in any meaningful sense is not a Republican. The registration records show that since 1987 Trump has been a Republican, then an independent, a Democrat, and then a Republican again. He has donated to both parties, but did not show any loyalty and affinity for either.[40] Underscoring how chaos is gripping the current political environment Rauch argued:

Chaos syndrome is a chronic decline in the political system's capacity for self-organization. It begins with the weakening of the institutions and brokers—political parties, career politicians, and congressional leaders and committees—

> that have historically held politicians accountable to one another and prevented everyone in the system from pursuing naked self-interest all the time. As these intermediaries' influence fades, politicians, activists, and voters all become more individualistic and unaccountable. The system atomizes. Chaos becomes the new normal—both in campaigns and in the government itself.[41]

Chaos in the political world, with more and more renegades calling the shots, might be emerging as the new norm, but what does it entail for journalism and journalists? What are the lessons to be learned from the 2016 presidential campaign? As the journalism community gets into the mode of introspection and retrospection a few aspects come to the fore. The mainstream media should reassess their coverage of political candidates, unconventional or otherwise, in the near future and shun their old practice of building up candidates, so they can tear them down. In this age of social media and Trump era, journalists should recommit to the first tenet of their professional ethics—seek truth and report it, even though it is easier said than done. The present day challenges for journalism are articulated well in Jamie Bartlett's piece on the internet and Trump:

> The internet is an overwhelming smorgasbord of competing facts, claims, blogs, data, propaganda, misinformation, investigative journalism, charts, different charts, commentary, and reportage. In our busy lives, and faced with this overwhelming choice, we will pay attention to the one person making more noise than anyone else. We only have time to click on that funny thing at the top of our feeds or check the thing everyone else is sharing and little time to worry about the details or long-winded arguments. "Post-truth politics" and "echo-chambers" have become a sort of stock response for people struggling to explain why politics isn't going their way: but they're just symptoms. We aren't past truth. It's has just been relegated relative to attention.[42]

In all this digital din the truth might be getting relegated relative to attention, but sustained effort should be made by the journalists to uncover and report the truth. Multi-pronged approach should be initiated to increase media literacy among citizenry enabling them to clearly decipher news from fake news. Journalists should continue to uphold their watchdog function. They should clearly understand that they are serving as the watchdogs for democracy and not for corporates or politicians.

NOTES

1. Thomas Patterson. "Pre-Primary News Coverage of the 2016 Presidential Race: Trump's Rise, Sanders' Emergence, Clinton's Struggle." Harvard Kennedy School's

Shorenstein Center on Media, Politics and Public Policy, June 13, 2016, https://shorensteincenter.org/pre-primary-news-coverage-2016-trump-clinton-sanders/; Julia R. Azari, 2016. "How the News Media Helped to Nominate Trump" *Political Communication* 33, no. 4: 677–680, *Communication & Mass Media Complete*, EBSCO*host* (accessed August 11, 2017).

2. Solomon Messing, and Sean J. Westwood, 2014, "Selective Exposure in the Age of Social Media: Endorsements Trump Partisan Source Affiliation when Selecting News Online," *Communication Research* 41, no. 8: 1042–1063, *Communication & Mass Media Complete*, EBSCO*host* (accessed August 11, 2017); John Parmelee. "Donald Trump, Reality TV, and the Political Power of Parasocial Relationships;" Electionanalysis2016.us, http://www.electionanalysis2016.us/us-election-analysis-2016/section-7-pop-culture-and-populism/donald-trump-reality-tv-and-the-political-power-of-parasocial-relationships/.

3. Thomas Patterson. "News Coverage of the 2016 General Election: How the Press Failed the Voters," Harvard Kennedy School's Shorenstein Center on Media, Politics and Public Policy, December 7, 2016, https://shorensteincenter.org/news-coverage-2016-general-election/.

4. Karen Callaghan, and Frauke Schnell, 2001, "Assessing the Democratic Debate: How the News Media Frame Elite Policy Discourse," *Political Communication* 18, no. 2: 183–213, *Communication & Mass Media Complete*, EBSCO*host* (accessed August 11, 2017).

5. Robert M. Entman. "Framing: Toward Clarification of a Fractured Paradigm," *Journal of communication* 43, no. 4 (1993): 51–58.

6. Maxwell Tani. "We Asked 11 Media Outlets How Their Coverage Has Changed since Trump's Election—Here's What They Said." *Business Insider*, February 5, 2017. http://www.businessinsider.com/media-trump-how-coverage-changed-election-2017–2.

7. Jonathan Rauch. "How American Politics Went Insane," *Atlantic*, last modified August 2016, https://www.theatlantic.com/magazine/archive/2016/07/how-american-politics-went-insane/485570./

8. Gianpietro Mazzoleni. "Did the Media Create Trump?" US election analysis 2016, http://www.electionanalysis2016.us/us-election-analysis-2016/section-1-media/did-the-media-create-trump/.

9. Ibid.

10. Ibid.

11. https://www.spj.org/ethicscode.asp.

12. Gallup Poll, "'Email' Dominates What Americans Have Heard about Clinton," Sept. 19, 2016, http://news.gallup.com/poll/195596/email-dominates-americans-heard-clinton.aspx.

13. Entman, "Framing: Toward Clarification," 52.

14. Parmelee, "Donald Trump, Reality TV, and the Political Power."

15. Paul Bond. "Leslie Moonves on Donald Trump: 'It May Not Be Good for America, but It's Damn Good for CBS.'" *The Hollywood Reporter*. Feb. 29, 2016, http://www.hollywoodreporter.com/news/leslie-moonves-donald-trump-may-871464.

16. Patterson, "Pre-Primary News Coverage."

17. James Poniewozik. "What 'The Apprentice' Taught Donald Trump about Campaigning," October 9, 2015, https://www.nytimes.com/2015/10/10/arts/television/donald-trump-campaign-the-apprentice.html.

18. Patterson, "Pre-Primary News Coverage."

19. Jeff Guo. "The Real Reasons Donald Trump's So Popular—for People Totally Confused by It," *Washington Post*, December 12, 2015. https://www.washingtonpost.com/news/wonk/wp/2015/12/12/the-four-basic-reasons-that-explain-why-donald-trump-actually-is-so-popular/.

20. Paul Bond. "Leslie Moonves on Donald Trump."

21. Ashley Parker and Amy Chozick. "Donald Trump's Act Seems to Be Wearing Out Its Welcome," October 7, 2017, https://www.nytimes.com/2015/10/08/us/politics/donald-trumps-bombast-seems-to-be-wearing-out-its-welcome.html.

22. Jack Shafer. "Trump isn't Media Creation."

23. Bill Kovach and Tom Rosenstiel. "Campaign Lite: Why Reporter's Won't Tell Us What We Need to Know," *Washington Monthly*, January/February 2001.

24. Thomas Patterson. News Coverage of the 2016 Presidential Primaries: Horse Race Reporting Has Consequences, July 11, 2016, https://shorensteincenter.org/news-coverage-2016-presidential-primaries/#_ftnref1.

25. Ibid.

26. Gianpietro Mazzoleni. "Did the Media Create Trump?"

27. Thomas Patterson. "News Coverage of the 2016 General Election."

28. Ibid.

29. Kenneth Campbell. "Did Election Results Trump Frames of Newspaper Endorsements?" US Election Analysis 2016, http://www.electionanalysis2016.us/us-election-analysis-2016/section-1-media/did-election-results-trump-frames-of-newspaper-endorsements/.

30. Thomas Patterson. "News Coverage of the 2016 General Election."

31. Ibid.

32. Pew Research Center, "Covering President Trump in a Polarized Media Environment," October 2, 2017, http://www.journalism.org/2017/10/02/covering-president-trump-in-a-polarized-media-environment/.

33. Pew Research Center, "In Trump's First 100 Days, News Stories Citing His Tweets Were More Likely to be Negative." October 18, 2017, http://www.pewresearch.org/fact-tank/2017/10/18/in-trumps-first-100-days-news-stories-citing-his-tweets-were-more-likely-to-be-negative/.

34. Pew Research Center, "Covering President Trump in a Polarized Media Environment."

35. Pew Research Center, "Early Coverage of the Trump Presidency Rarely Included Citizen Voices, October 4, 2017," http://www.pewresearch.org/fact-tank/2017/10/04/early-coverage-of-the-trump-presidency-rarely-included-citizen-voices/.

36. Pew Research Center, "Covering President Trump in a Polarized Media Environment."

37. Maxwell Tani. "We asked 11 media outlets."

38. Reuters, "Covering Trump the Reuters Way," January 31, 2017, http://www.reuters.com/article/rpb-adlertrump/covering-trump-the-reuters-way-idUSKBN15F276.

39. Jonathan Rauch. "How American Politics Went Insane."

40. Ibid.

41. Ibid.

42. Jamie Bartlett. "The Utopian Dream of the Internet Has Become a Nightmare."

Chapter Three

"A Statement from the President"

The Social Construction of News and Journalists' Use of Donald Trump's Tweets

Brian Moritz

On June 1, 2017, a new Twitter account opened, calling itself Real Press Sec. @RealPressSecBot is an automated account created by Pat Cunnane and Russell Neiss.[1] Each time President Donald Trump tweets from his verified personal account (@RealDonaldTrump), the Real Press Sec. Twitter account sends out a tweet of its own, with the exact wording of Trump's tweet, only formatted to appear like a "Statement by the President" on official White House letterhead.

The Real Press Sec. account takes the 140-character statements issued by President Trump and transforms them into official looking announcements from the President of the United States. The effect is quite stunning when you consider that Trump's tweets denouncing CNN and the *New York Times* as "fake news," or "garbage journalism," or his attack on MSNBC host Mika Brzezinski's appearance ("She was bleeding badly from a facelift"), are not presented in the traditional format of a tweet, rather in the stark, simple, black and white print of a press release statement.[2] The Real Press Sec. provides a gravity to President Trump's tweets, treating them not as ephemeral internet messages, but instead as official public statements from the president of the United States.

The Twitter account highlights one of the most interesting dilemmas facing reporters. Donald Trump has been a prolific Twitter user predating his announcement as a candidate for president in 2015 and before he won the 2016 election. Between November 9, 2016—the day after he became president-elect—and July 1, 2017, Trump tweeted 1,263 times over these 235 days, averaging more than five tweets per day. He leveraged this social media platform to attack political rivals, threaten the news media, and even announce a change in military policy regarding the enlistment of transgender soldiers.

The official White House Twitter feed (@WhiteHouse) started in 2007, and Barack Obama was the first president to actively use Twitter in office. But Trump's use of the social network and 140-character messages has challenged journalistic norms. Are tweets from the president official statements? Are they considered public policy statements? Could a president potentially pardon himself or anybody with a tweet? Are presidential tweets automatically worthy of coverage by journalists?

This topic has produced a great deal of debate within journalism trade publications and blogs since the first months of the Trump administration. Kramer, writing for the Poynter Institute, suggests that reporters should always provide context for the president's tweets in the form of a checklist so readers are able to see when the tweet was sent, who it was about, and why it may have been sent.[3] Additionally, Pope from the *Columbia Journalism Review* argues that media obsessed too much about Trump's tweets—particularly ones that attacked the media.[4] "We aren't obligated to cede the media agenda to this or any other administration. We control the airtime, we decide who gets quoted and how, we set the rules of engagement."[5] Hess of the *New York Times* wrote that President Trump's use of Twitter has, in many ways, redefined the platform.[6] "Twitter is his vice. And after eight years of straight-as-an-arrow posts from @BarackObama, equally Twitter-obsessed journalists are transfixed by Mr. Trump's timeline, too."[7]

There is an easy, top-of-mind answer to the questions presented above. It is the argument of prominence, long considered a core value within journalism and news reporting. Donald Trump is the president of the United States. Tweets are public statements, able to be read by anyone with internet access. What the president says in public is newsworthy. End of story. But it is worth examining each part of this assumption to better understand the complexity of the issue.

The social construction of news is a key concept in the study of news and journalism. If news is created by the routines, practices, and values of journalists, then to understand those is to understand news itself.[8] The work of a generation of media sociology scholars has shown how news is constructed, as well as the consequences of that process.

The social construction of news is a loosely coupled theoretical notion that examines how news is constructed. Berkowitz and Shoemaker and Reese, among other scholars, note that news *can* be considered a social construct.[9] A review of literature on the topic examines how news is developed. Tuchman found that news is not a reflection of reality (as the traditional journalistic ethos holds) but instead a construction of reality; which is made by journalists through their routines.[10] News is a social construct, something that is created through journalistic norms, attitudes, practices, and routines.[11] Gans wrote that news construction is a complex interplay of journalists' attitudes and practices, and organizational goals and constraints.[12]

While many of the landmark studies in this field date back to the 1960s and 1970s—a time before the widespread use of computers, much less the internet and Twitter—they still provide insights into understanding how news is made in the digital and social media age. The routines of journalism are deeply embedded within the profession, whether it is viewed as an organizational field or a community of actors.[13] Examining the historical roots of the social construction of news and applying them to the contemporary news environment will help us understand and answer the questions posed by the writers in modern trade publications—what is the proper way to cover President Trump's tweets? Why do journalists rely on these often outlandish statements that are at best provocative and at worst provocative, racist, and distracting from other world issues in their stories?

Understanding journalism routines, particularly the relationship between journalists and sources—will help us see how and why journalists use Trump's tweets in their reporting. "Knowing how the news gets made—the organization and politics of news making—is a prerequisite for understanding what the news means."[14]

To accomplish this, we will look at three facets of the social construction of news and how they relate to the use of Trump's tweets. First, the ways journalists use official sources in their stories will be examined. Then, the idea of news channels will be addressed. Finally, the idea of news values will be used to determine why Trump's tweets are used in journalism.

OFFICIAL SOURCES

It is virtually impossible to discuss journalism without discussing the relationship between a journalists and their sources. "What the news is depends very much on who its sources are."[15]

Reporters can't be everywhere. They can't be there when a car accident happens or when a murder takes place or when a decision on which football player to draft in the first round is made. Therefore, they are reliant upon sources for their information. Any study of journalism is primarily a study of sources.[16] While these sources can include documents (both public and private) and databases, sources are primarily people. Sigal noted that journalism can be defined as what a source says has happened or what will happen.[17] Gans compared the journalist-source relationship to a dance and that the source is always leading.[18] Sigal used a different metaphor, saying that reporters have cameras but the sources are the light source.[19] Without sources, journalists have little or no news to report. "Journalism, on a day-to-day basis, is the story of the interaction of reporters and government officials, both politicians and bureaucrats. Most analysts claim officials have the upper hand."[20]

The identity of these sources is important to consider as well. Sigal, Gans, Fishman, and Tuchman, among others, noted that all journalists rely more on official sources—primarily official government sources—than anyone else for their news.[21] Journalists tend to focus their reporting on sources in the centers of power, most prominently the White House.[22] This reliance on sources occurs for several reasons. For one, government sources are socially sanctioned, and they have power and access to information. If a police officer gives details about a crime, there's a certain social acceptance given to that description over an ordinary person's description (or especially the accused's version of events).[23] Official sources also hold a place of privilege for reporters because they are regular, reliable sources of news. Government officials hold regular press conferences. Courts are open to the public and transcripts are available.

As for journalists, there is no bigger source than the president of the United States. Covering the White House is viewed as the most prestigious beat possible for a news reporter in a large part because reporters are covering the president.[24]

In his landmark study of news, Gans described the importance of the president to reporters.[25] If the actions of the federal government are the most newsworthy, Gans wrote, it follows that the president is the most important actor on the most important stage.

> He and, even more so, those who can speak for him or the White House are almost always and easily accessible. . . . The president is thus also the most productive source of news. At the same time, he is deemed the most authoritative and reliable—if not always trustworthy—source, as well as the best-known and most prestigious. The president is a particularly suitable source for national news because he is thought to be "speaking for the country," as one editor put it; and according to an executive producer: "For all practical purposes, he is the country." . . . "The president is also source for the biggest story of all. As a Washington bureau chief once told me: 'We cover the president expecting he will die.'"[26]

Despite early thoughts that Twitter could revolutionize journalism by giving more attention to other voices, the way journalists use Twitter has comported with established norms and practices. The reliance on official government sources remains a key journalistic routine, merely moving from the phone or the briefing room to Twitter.[27] "Mainstream media relied more on the Twitter feeds of traditional official sources than on those of non-official sources."[28] The White House is still viewed as a prestigious beat, and the president the most official of all official sources.

Interestingly, a journalist's relationship to the president is different than virtually any other source. A reporter can't simply call the president and get a quote, as is typical for a mayor or a high-school football coach. Presidential interviews are events, ones that are rarely granted and treated as special.[29] The public statements from the president and the White House are often very polished, very on-message, very hermetically sealed. In this regard, President Trump's Twitter feed is a bonanza for journalists. It is a rare glimpse into the real-time thoughts of the most powerful man in the world. Journalist Mark Leibovich wrote in the *New York Times* that President Trump said in an interview that an unnamed "they" wanted him to stop using Twitter; something the president said he had no intention of doing. "The tweets were becoming a growing topic of concern among Republicans, many of whom were urging him to stop," Leibovich wrote. "But like most reporters, I found his tweets far more illuminating than anything the White House press office could ever disgorge. I urged him to keep it up."[30]

NEWS CHANNELS

News channels can be best understood as the places journalists get their news. If news comes from sources, then channels are how that information is delivered from source to journalist. A source is an individual that provides the raw materials of news. The channel is the means by which those raw materials are delivered.

In a study of reporters and government officials in Washington DC, Leon Sigal found that news comes from three distinct channels—routine channels, informal channels, and enterprise channels.[31] Sigal defined routine channels as things like official proceedings, press releases, press conferences, and nonspontaneous events (such as speeches, ceremonies, staged demonstrations). Informal channels are defined as things like leaks, briefings that happen on background (where the source is not speaking for attribution), stories taken from other news outlets, and nongovernmental proceedings. Enterprise channels, as defined by Sigal, are primarily ones where the reporter initiates the work (either an interview conducted on her own or data research a journalist conducts of his own volition), conclusions or analysis from a reporter, or spontaneous events, such as fires, riots, natural disasters that a reporter witnesses first hand.

Sigal found that 71.8 percent of the news produced by reporters in Washington DC comes via routine channels. While this certainly opens up areas of criticism for reporters, studies into the social construction of news do not tend to suggest anything nefarious about this. In fact, the research has shown that it's often merely the way the job work.

Routine channels are an important part of daily journalism and they are tied to the beat structure. A beat is where a reporter is assigned to regularly cover an organization or a geographic entity and produce daily stories from their beat. Fishman demonstrated how news work is bureaucratically organized for reporters through the beat structure and reliance on official sources.[32]

Fishman also found that the beat is bureaucratically structured to provide the journalist with access to the right sources of reliable, socially sanctioned information.[33] A cops reporter, for example, has access to the daily blotter, press conferences, press releases, and to interviews with officers if need be. A city hall reporter has access to the mayor, the mayor's spokesperson, legislators, and other public employees (along with public records). Fishman described this as the beat round, in which a reporter will visit the key offices on his or her beat, chatting with people (both on and off the record, both officials and secretaries) and collecting information. What's important to note in the beat round is what's missing: the public. What's present in the beat round is the officially sanctioned side of the story, and that's what journalists are exposed to.

Additionally, Fishman found that beat reporters are obliged to write a story every day, regardless of whether anything is happening. Calling back to the office and saying "nothing's going on, no story today" is simply not an acceptable practice. That puts the reporter under pressure to find something to write about every day, regardless of whether it is important to the public. This need for a daily story also ties into Tuchman's notions of the "news net." Tuchman characterized news work through the "news net," which journalists cast out every day to find stories.[34] Rather than a news blanket, which would cover everything, Tuchman refers to it as a net because it is focused on the big fish and lets little fish slip through, and is focused on official sources of news, and official happenings of public figures and business leaders; often ignoring what happens to non-official, everyday folk.

This is not meant as a criticism of journalists. Every job has its routines. The point of routines is to do work in the easiest and most efficient way. Put colloquially, reporters have a job to do (write/produce a story every day from their beat) and relying on routine channels allows them to do so efficiently. But just because it is an understandable practice doesn't mean there are not implications. "Newsmen, by adhering to routine channels of news gathering, leave much of the talk of selection of stories to their sources."[35]

This has not changed much in the age of digital and social journalism. Indeed, the development of digital journalism in many ways can be seen as the combination of print traditions and online technologies. "Online newspapers have emerged by merging print's unidirectional and text-based traditions with networked computing's interactive and (more recently) multimedia potentials."[36]

One example of this process is normalization, which occurs when journalists adapt a new media format to the existing norms, values, and practices of news work. In her seminal study of journalism blogs during the 2004 U.S. presidential election, Singer found journalists were taking a media format that originated as personal, online diaries and normalizing them, infusing them with journalism's professional norms and ideals.[37] The journalists, Singer found, also were not using blogs to bring in outside voices but instead were creating a sort of news echo chamber in which they cited other media outlets (often fellow traditional media outlets) rather than elicit audience members' reactions.

Using Singer's notion of normalization as a framework, Lasorsa, Lewis, and Horton examined how journalists use Twitter.[38] Like Singer six years earlier, Lasorsa and his colleagues found that reporters were normalizing Twitter, adopting the rules of journalistic norms and practices into their use of the microblogging platform. They also found that reporters were adapting some of their norms and practices to the conventions of Twitter—most notably the use of opinion within tweets. Taken together, the Singer and Lasorsa, Lewis, and Horton studies suggest that when a new communication platform emerges, journalists are predisposed to normalize it, to take the new media form and shape it to fit existing norms, practices, and routines rather than allow those practices to evolve to fit the new format. This represents one of the central tensions that social media platforms, especially Twitter, has brought to daily journalism. These platforms present new ways to report the news and engage with audiences, potentially moving beyond the traditional journalistic paradigm—but news organizations and individual journalists still tend to use new platforms not to their full potential, but rather in conventional ways.

But in some ways, as early as 2010, it was clear that Twitter was beginning to at least partially redefine some journalism routines and practices.[39] This included the use of Twitter as an official channel for news. When a political leader or other public figure tweets a statement, journalists are able to treat that as an official news channel and quote it directly in their stories. It's within this context that President Trump's tweets are taken by journalists as more than just 140-character statements on a social media platform. They are official public statements by a public figure (and now, a public official).

In a way, it is win-win. It allows the politician or celebrity to control the statement they issue publicly on an issue and communicate it directly to a wide audience. It gives journalists instant and immediate access to their sources, delivering a quote or statement they can use in stories right to their computers or smartphones. This may be a growing challenge in journalism given both access to sources and the routines and practices of young reporters who grew up with social media platforms as part of their work. One study suggests that, among younger journalists (five or fewer years of professional experience), contacting sources was the most stressful part of their job—in large part, because they relied on email to communicate with sources, whereas more experienced reporters relied on the telephone.[40]

A 2014 study showed that Twitter was used as a source in more than half of the stories studied (both TV news and newspapers), and that TV news relied on Twitter as a primary source much more than newspapers.[41] The president (in this study, Barack Obama), or other officials within the executive branch, had tweets quoted in 19.6 percent of stories that included Twitter as a primary source. Members of Congress' Twitter feeds were quoted in 47.2 percent of stories in the sample.[42] This suggests that Twitter is an updated version of a routine channel, defined by Sigal more than forty years ago. Twitter cannot be viewed as another media outlet because it is much more of a platform for individuals and publishers to make public comments (so it is not an informal channel) and because it is not of the reporters' own initiative, it is not an enterprise channel. Because Twitter is a routine channel, it is favored by journalists—which means that, along with the identity of the source, the nature of it is another reason President Trump's tweets are used in news stories. "Journalists were found to maintain the professional routines formed to achieve the highest efficiency of the organizations, even when employing Twitter as a news source. Journalists still throw their news nets to the same spots as they did in the pre-Internet age."[43]

The social construction of news includes what Høyer and Pöttker defined as the journalism paradigm.[44] They defined five aspects of the western journalism paradigm—news value (rather than political bias), a 24-hour news cycle, the use of the news interview, the inverted-pyramid style of writing (in which the most important facts are put at the top of the story), and objectivity.

Three of these aspects can be seen in how reporters use Trump's tweets. They fit predetermined news values (as defined above). They fit perfectly into the 24-hour news cycle. In fact, a number of Trump's tweets come early in the morning—a time of the 24-hour news cycle that is traditionally slower than other times, so they create news at a time that is usually a bit of a vacuum. They also fit into the idea of a news interview. Rather than a traditional in-person interview, the tweets stand in as a sort of proxy interview with the most powerful person in the world—an interview that is delivered directly to a reporter's computer or phone, 140-characters at a time (table 3.1).

Table 3.1. Timetable of President Trump's Tweets in a News Cycle

Elements of Journalism Paradigm	*President Trump's Tweets*
24-hour news cycle	Are published at all hours. Many come early in the morning (Eastern time), a time when there is traditionally little news made.
News Values	Prominence, Deviance, the product of traditional sources and the traditional news net.
News Interview	A proxy for an actual, in-person interview—one that can be quoted directly and that is delivered directly to a reporter's phone or computer.

JOURNALISM PARADIGM AND PRESIDENT TRUMP'S TWEETS

An example of this can be seen on July 25, 2017, when President Trump sent two tweets that were critical of the perceived in action by his attorney general, Jeff Sessions, to investigate alleged crimes by Hillary Clinton, Trump's opponent in the 2016 presidential election.[45] President Trump sent the tweets at 6:03 a.m. and 6:12 a.m., leading to coverage of the tweets as a major story that day. These tweets are a part of the 24-hour news cycle—coming at 6 a.m., when government offices aren't generally open to the public and morning news shows are recapping the previous days events, they gave fresh material to journalists at a time of day when there is usually little new news to report and set the agenda for that day's reporting. They demonstrate both proximity and deviance, as defined later in this chapter—both in their content (the president criticizing his own attorney general) and the timing (much of the coverage stressed the early morning timing of the tweets). And the tweets were all cited directly, the same way a quote from the president in a speech or press conference would have been cited. Therefore, the tweets acted as a proxy interview.

NEWS VALUES

The source and the channel are important parts of the social construction of news. But journalists talk to many sources throughout their day, and an incredible amount of information comes to them through formal, informal, and enterprise channels. The final step in creating the news is the application of news values. These are the characteristics that journalists and editors apply to information to determine whether or not they should be written about. This is where reporters and editors call something "news worthy."

To professional journalists, news is something that exists out there in the world, and it's a reporter's job to go out there and find it. News is something to be discovered. That is a core belief of the news paradigm. The sociological view holds that news is not something that exists in the world but is in fact a social construct. But one thing the two views have in common is the application of news values.

This sentiment applies to what Becker and Vlad refer to as story ideation.[46] Story ideation is the process by which reporters and editors come up with stories—what stories are covered, how they are covered, and how they are played within a publication. Becker and Vlad call this the most important part of the journalism process, because it is from these decisions that all other acts of journalism flow.

The social construction of news is not meant to suggest that reporters make up the news. The concept of the social construction of news simply means that news is created daily by a socially agreed-upon collection of norms, values, and practices that journalists call newsworthiness. Schudson defined several elements of news, including the fact that it is usually event-driven, negative, process-driven (rather than results driven), and reflects the world and points of view of official sources.[47] Shoemaker defined news values as including deviance, timeliness, proximity, and impact.[48]

Prominence

Another well-established news value is known as prominence.[49] Prominence is when an event happens to a person of elevated social status. The more elevated that person's social status, the more likely that event will become news. A man having lunch at a small bistro on Park Avenue in Rochester, New York, is no one's idea of a news story—but it was in 2014, when President Obama did just that.[50] A college student lying about a romantic relationship is hardly front-page news—but it was in 2011, when that student was Manti T'eo, a Heisman trophy candidate playing for the University of Notre Dame.[51] Britney Spears shaving her head was a tabloid story for days, whereas me shaving my head would merely be a poor life choice mocked by my friends and loved ones. The point is that the actions of certain people are more likely to be considered newsworthy by journalists than those of others. And few people are more prominent in the United States than the president.

As introduced earlier in the chapter in the discussion on official sources, the president is seen as a source of unique prominence. He is arguably the most powerful person in the world. His words can impact the stock market and, by extension, the global economy. His statements can provoke potential military action. He is the commander in chief of the world's most powerful military force, and he alone has the authority to launch nuclear weapons.

The president, in many ways, defines the news value of prominence. So, the statements he makes, even on Twitter, are seen as potentially newsworthy on their face.

But news values and news judgment don't end merely with prominence. For something to be news, it's not merely enough for it to be spoken by a prominent person. Plenty of high-profile people make statements and do things every day, and they are not automatically covered on the news. In a reporter's eyes, there must be something else there. Sometimes, this is timeliness—it is about an issue or even that is happening now. Sometimes, it is proximity—something happening in a reader's hometown is more newsworthy than something happening four states away. Sometimes, it is impact—a flood may always be news, but a flood that destroys large portions of a city or results in deaths has a greater impact and so is more newsworthy.

Often times, that something is called deviance.

Deviance

In the social construction of news, deviance is something outside the accepted, normal boundaries of everyday life, notes Shoemaker, Chang, and Bredlinger.[52] In the simplest terms, this is the "Man Bites Dog" idea of news judgment. When things go as expected, or things happen as we think they are supposed to, that is not considered very newsworthy. When things out of the ordinary happen, reporters are more likely to judge them as newsworthy. This makes a certain amount of common sense. A story headlined "Plane lands safely after routine flight" would not qualify as news. "Plane lands safely in Hudson river shortly after takeoff" was one of the biggest stories of 2011.[53]

Pam Shoemaker has done the most important work on deviance throughout her career. She theorized that humans are hard-wired to search their environment for deviance as a survival mechanism dating back to hunter-gatherer times (as a pure survival mechanism), and that remained with us through evolution.[54] Deviance is often seen as a dominant news value, because dating back to traveling minstrels, deviance is what people want to hear about. Stories about things going well or not changing are not as interesting to people as stories about people acting in deviant ways.

> Today's entertainment and social media emphasize deviance through their tendency to include violence, as well as interpersonal conflict, celebrity gossip, and oddity. In the social media, people are more likely to communicate the worrisome or unusual parts of their day rather than what was boring and dull. For both news media and social media organizations, surveillance of the environment for

deviance is an important routine activity, but not the only force that determines whether an event becomes news.[55]

If nothing else, Donald Trump's Twitter feed is a study in deviance.

No other political has used the platform the way he has. Most politicians use it for rather banal public statements or partisan comments aimed at generating support from their supporters. Occasionally, they may post the occasional zinger. But President Trump's Twitter feed is something else. He uses it to openly criticize the news media (referring to mainstream outlets who report on him and his administration as Fake News, consistently referring to the "failing" *New York Times* and the "Amazon" *Washington Post*), insult TV personalities, criticize the on-going investigation into his campaign's connections to the Vladimir Putin's Russian government (including calling his own attorney general beleaguered), suggest a change in military policy disparage other countries' foreign policies, and more.

Remember, too, this all happened in the first six months of his administration.

By any definition, President Trump's tweets are an example of deviance as a news value.

CONCLUSION

At the start of this chapter, it was posited that there was a very simple explanation for the reason that President Donald Trump's tweets were considered so newsworthy by journalists—What the president says in public is newsworthy. Certainly, that is the case. "Mr. Trump expertly exploits journalists' unwavering attention to their Twitter feeds, their competitive spirit and their ingrained journalistic conventions—chiefly, that what the president says is inherently newsworthy."[56]

But this chapter has demonstrated that there is much more to it than that. This chapter has shown that the core elements of the social construction of news explain how reporters use President Trump's tweets. Understanding the social construction of news helps us see why journalists feel they cannot simply ignore the president's tweets, no matter how offensive they may be to some communities or how some observers feel they are designed to distract the media and the public from other more serious issues.[57] The social construction of news provides a lens through which we can understand why journalists act the way they do about Trump's tweets. They are not being driven solely by a desire for a ratings and page views, nor are they being played by a master manipulator. The use of the president's tweets is deeply embedded in the established norms and practices of daily journalism. Tweets are considered public statements, and public statements—especially those made by public officials like the president—can be quoted in news stories. The fact that they appear on a social media platform is irrelevant. The format doesn't matter. Journalism is what sources tell journalists, and the president of the United States is one of the most important sources of news in our society. His public statements—whether in a Rose Garden press conference, a speech from the Oval Office or a post on Twitter—are considered newsworthy by journalists because he is a source. The fact that he often says things that are surprising or shocking—at least compared with our expectations for president—adds to this newsworthiness.

Twitter also provides journalists with a new official channel of news from the president and from other government officials and agencies. Journalists have long relied on official channels, not out of allegiance to the ruling elite but because of a sense of bureaucratic efficiency. Reporters have to write stories from their beats every day. President Trump making a statement on Twitter provides reporters with information through an official channel that is delivered directly to their phones or computers. In this regard, a tweet is no different than a press release or a formal statement. This is what makes the Real Press Sec. account on Twitter so effective—it takes what could be viewed as an ephemeral statement and makes it look like what journalists believe it is: a statement from the president.

In a very real sense, Trump's tweets are a perfect journalist storm. They are public statements coming from a prominent official source. They come through a routine channel, one that is in fact delivered directly to their computers or smartphones. Their content is often deviant, a core news value. It's not surprising that journalists use them so often and that they are a core part of the coverage of the forty-fifth president's administration.

NOTES

1. Hayley Jones, "This Twitter Bot Turns Trump's Tweets into Official Press Secretary Releases. It Is Brilliant," Thedailybeast.com, June 5, 2017, http://www.thedailybeast.com/this-twitter-bot-turns-trumps-tweets-into-official-press-secretary-releases-it-is-brilliant.

2. Donald Trump, "Donald J. Trump on Twitter: '. . . to Mar-a-Lago 3 Nights in a Row around New Year's Eve, and Insisted on Joining Me. She Was Bleeding Badly From a Face-Lift. I Said No!'" Twitter Post, June 29, 2017, https://twitter.com/realDonaldTrump/status/880410114456465411.

3. Melody Kramer, "Here's How to Cover President Trump's Tweets," Poynter.org, February 8, 2017, http://www.poynter.org/2017/heres-how-news-organizations-should-cover-president-trumps-tweets/448160/.

4. Kyle Pope, "What We Miss when We Obsess over Trump's Tweets," July 5, 2017, https://www.cjr.org/covering_trump/trump_tweets_press_journalists.php.

5. Ibid.

6. Amanda Hess, "Trump, Twitter and the Art of His Deal," *New York Times*, January 15, 2017.

7. Ibid.

8. Pamela J Shoemaker and Stephen D Reese, *Mediating the Message in the 21st Century*, (Routledge, 2013).

9. Daniel A Berkowitz, *Social Meanings of News*, (SAGE, 1997); Shoemaker and Reese, *Mediating the Message in the 21st Century*.

10. Gaye Tuchman, *Making News*, (New York: Free Press, 1980).

11. Mark Fishman, *Manufacturing the News* (Austin: University of Texas Press, 1980).

12. Herbert J Gans, *Deciding What's News* (Evanston, IL: Northwestern University Press, 1979).

13. Barbie Zelizer, "Journalists as Interpretive Communities," *Critical Studies in Media Communication* 10, no. 3 (May 18, 2009): 219–237, doi:10.1080/15295039309366865.

14. Leon V Sigal, *Reporters and Officials*, (Washington, DC: DC Heath, 1973), 187.

15. Ibid., 189.

16. Paul Manning, *News and News Sources*, (Thousand Oaks, CA: SAGE, 2001).

17. Sigal, *Reporters and Officials*.

18. Gans, *Deciding What's News*.

19. Sigal, *Reporters and Officials*.

20. Ibid., 142.

21. Ibid.; Gans, *Deciding What's News*; Fishman, *Manufacturing the News*; Tuchman, *Making News*.

22. D. Charles Whitney et al., "Geographic and Source Biases in Network Television News 1982–1984," *Journal of Broadcasting & Electronic Media* 33, no. 2 (May 18, 1989): 159–174, doi:10.1080/08838158909364070.

23. Fishman, *Manufacturing the News*.

24. Whitney et al., "Geographic and Source Biases in Network Television News 1982–1984."

25. Gans, *Deciding What's News*.

26. Ibid.

27. Steven Livingston and W. Lance Bennett, "Gatekeeping, Indexing, and Live-Event News: Is Technology Altering the Construction of News?," *Political Communication* 20, no. 4 (June 24, 2003): 363–380, doi:10.1080/10584600390244121.

28. Soo Jung Moon and Patrick Hadley, "Routinizing a New Technology in the Newsroom: Twitter as a News Source in Mainstream Media," *Journal of Broadcasting & Electronic Media* 58, no. 2 (June 5, 2014): 289–305, doi:10.1080/08838151.2014.906435.

29. Michael Schudson, *The Sociology of News* (New York: W. W. Norton, 2011).

30. Mark Leibovich, "This Town Melts Down," *New York Times*, July 11, 2017.

31. Sigal, *Reporters and Officials*.
32. Fishman, *Manufacturing the News*.
33. Ibid.
34. Tuchman, *Making News*.
35. Sigal, *Reporters and Officials*, 130.
36. Pablo J. Boczkowski, *Digitizing the News* (Cambridge, MA: MIT Press, 2005), 4.
37. Jane B. Singer, "The Political J-Blogger," *Journalism* 6, no. 2 (June 29, 2005): 173–198, doi:10.1177/1464884905051009.
38. Dominic L. Lasorsa, Seth C. Lewis, and Avery E. Holton, "Normalizing Twitter," *Journalism Studies* 13, no. 1 (April 21, 2011): 19–36, doi:10.1080/1461670X.2011.571825.
39. Alfred Hermida, "Twittering the News," *Journalism Practice* 4, no. 3 (August 2010): 297–308, doi:10.1080/17512781003640703.
40. Signe Ivask, Heleri All, and Kairi Janson, "Time-Efficient and Time-Consuming Practices among Journalists in Communicating with the Sources," *Catalan Journal of Communication & Cultural Studies* 9, no. 1 (April 1, 2017): 25–41, doi:10.1386/cjcs.9.1.25_1.
41. Moon and Hadley, "Routinizing a New Technology in the Newsroom: Twitter as a News Source in Mainstream Media."
42. Ibid.
43. Ibid., 302.
44. S. Høyer and H. Pöttker, *Diffusion of the News Paradigm 1850–2000*, Nordicom 2005.
45. Jennifer Calfas, "President Trump Tweets Attorney General Jeff Sessions Is 'Very Weak' on Hillary Clinton," Time.com, July 25, 2017, http://time.com/4872242/trump-tweet-sessions-hillary-clinton/.
46. Jens Beckert, "Institutional Isomorphism Revisited: Convergence and Divergence in Institutional Change," *Sociological Theory* 28, no. 2 (June 1, 2010): 150–166, doi:10.1111/j.1467–9558.2010.01369.x.
47. Schudson, *The Sociology of News*.
48. P. J. Shoemaker, *Communication Concepts 3: Gatekeeping*, (Newsbury Park, London: Sage, 1991).
49. Robert Lloyd and Glenn Guzzo, *Writing and Reporting the News as a Story*, (Boston: Pearson College Division, 2009).
50. David Jackson, "Obama Stops at Rochester, N.Y., Deli," *USA Today*, August 22, 2013.
51. Timothy Burke and Jack Dickey, "Manti Te'O's Dead Girlfriend, the Most Heartbreaking and Inspirational Story of the College Football Season, Is a Hoax," Deadspin.com, January 16, 2013, http://deadspin.com/manti-teos-dead-girlfriend-the-most-heartbreaking-an-5976517.
52. P. J. Shoemaker and T. K. Chang, "Deviance as a Predictor of Newsworthiness: Coverage of International Events in the U.S. Media," *Annals of the International Communication Association* 10, no. 1 (1987) 348–65.
53. "N.Y. Jet Crash Called 'Miracle on the Hudson,'" *New York Daily News*, January 15, 2009.

54. Pamela Shoemaker. "Hardwired for News: Using Biological and Cultural Evolution to Explain the Surveillance Function." *Journal of Communication* 46, no. 3 (1996): 32–47.

55. Shoemaker and Reese, *Mediating the Message in the 21st Century*, 242.

56. Hess, "Trump, Twitter and the Art of His Deal."

57. Pope, "What We Miss when We Obsess over Trump's Tweets."

Part II

GOVERNMENT

Chapter Four

China Is Laughing at Us. SAD!

Trump's Twitter Diplomacy

Chiaoning Su and Paige L. Gibson

Every presidency is marked in some way by its relationship to emerging communication technologies. From Franklin D. Roosevelt's radio fireside chats, to Dwight D. Eisenhower's White House TV studio, to Ronald Reagan's live, prime time news conferences, to Barack Obama's social media engagement, presidents find opportunities in the latest technologies to fulfill their duties as chief diplomat. This relationship is clearest in moments of crisis.

On October 16, 1962, John F. Kennedy received intelligence about Soviet missiles being assembled for installation in Cuba. On October 22, Kennedy notified the American public via television broadcast of the presence of the missiles and his decision to ready the United States for possible military action. This means Kennedy had six days with his advisers to quietly and rationally work through the options away from public view. Throughout the crisis, U.S. and Soviet Union leaders relied on letters and other communications to diffuse the situation and achieve political agreement. The crisis ended on October 28, and a year later a direct telephone hotline was installed between the White House and the Kremlin.[1] Fifty-five years later, a similar threat faced the United States, but this crisis was defined by a very different communication technology.

Between July 8 and 29, 2017, President Trump used Twitter as a digital diplomat to encourage China to defuse the growing threats of a nuclear North Korea. President Trump's first tweet, on the second day of the G20 Summit, was full of promise: "Leaving Hamburg for Washington, D.C. and the WH. Just left China's President Xi where we had an excellent meeting on trade & North Korea."[2] However, twenty-one days later, Trump dramatically shifted his tone with two back to back tweets: "I am very disappointed in China. Our foolish past leaders have allowed them to make hundreds of billions of dollars a year in trade, yet . . . they do NOTHING for us with North Korea, just talk. We will no longer allow this to continue. China could easily solve this problem!"[3] In response to this outburst, China's state news agency Xinhua[4] published an editorial on July 31, stating its position on this issue: "Trump is quite a personality and he likes to tweet, however emotional venting cannot become the guidance for solving the nuclear issues on the Korean peninsula." The article also stressed China's efforts to maintain the peace in this region over the years, asked that China not be used as a scapegoat, and proposed a solution, that is for the United States and North Korea to both stop their military threats against one another.

This chapter examines Trump's use of social media in shaping an international reality and its potential for foreign policy formation. Based on a content analysis of Trump's 433 tweets on China, we first investigate a variety of topical, rhetorical, and structural constructions used by Trump to conjure a specific image of China for his followers. This image was supported by four frames, namely the *competitor*, the *nemesis*, the *weapon*, and the *irresponsible leader*. Secondly, we focus on Trump's tweets on Taiwan and its violation of the "One China Policy" protocol. Using in-depth textual analysis to read the subsequent coverage in five newspapers, including *New York Times*, *Washington Post*, *Los Angeles Times*, *Wall Street Journal*, and *Chicago Tribune*, we explore the interplay between social media and traditional media in the realm of international relations. Our findings demonstrate the complexity of US-China-Taiwan relations and the opportunities and challenges of foreign policy negotiation in the era of social media.

MEDIA AND INTERNATIONAL RELATIONS

Many continue to believe sensational press (the competition between Joseph Pulitzer's *World* and William Hurst's *New York Journal*) drove the United States into war with Spain in 1898.[5] Despite this notable example, international relations (IR) scholars were slow to recognize and examine the role of media in their research.[6]

Inspired by the realism paradigm of ancient Greece and ancient China, the classic international relations approach views states as the primary actors in an international system always in a state of anarchy.[7] These realists considered media a dangerous distraction to policy-makers' rational decision making and thus not an influence on state power but rather at best propagandistic tools to be wielded on others.[8] Media were more directly addressed in the later traditions of liberalism and constructivism. The classical liberal theory, inspired by the Enlightenment, looks to establish a moral standard for international systems, driven by justice not power.[9] Liberals emphasize the role of media as an effective influence on state action, both domestically and internationally.[10] Constructivist approaches to IR are rooted in the Frankfurt School and engage the symbolic aspects of socialization both within and between societies.[11] Here, media work with ideas and discourses to construct an international reality.[12]

The most prominent IR engagement of media arose in the 1990s in the form of the CNN effect.[13] By the 1990s, media forcefully inserted themselves into the discussion of international relations and foreign policy formation.[14] With its innovative use of satellites to relay world events to audiences in real time in a 24-hour news cycle, CNN established its dominance in global news production, remapped the media landscape, and made themselves arbiters of the foreign agenda.

Scholars amazed by media power during the first Persian Gulf War, in which CNN used embedded journalists to broadcast the whole war live, initiated more focused investigations of media effects on foreign policy formation and humanitarian interventions, thus coined the concept of CNN effect.[15] The CNN effect borrows from both liberalism and constructivism as it discusses the role of media in informing policy-makers' decision making and forging the mediated construction of an international reality, respectively.

While CNN is a prime example, the CNN effect goes beyond the named institution to suggest media influence international politics by way of media discourse and public opinion. According to Seib,[16] the CNN effect refers to "the dynamic tension that exists between real-time television news and policy-making, with the news having the upper hand in terms of influence." Livingston further differentiated the CNN effect into three interrelated media effects on political decision making: media as "agenda-setter," media as "accelerant," and media as "impediment" through which televised 24-hour real-time news direct policy-makers' attention, demand real-time responses, and use emotional appeals to muddle public support and disrupt military operations.[17]

Despite its dramatic and necessary shift in media politics, the CNN effect has been greatly criticized for lacking empirical support.[18] In the absence of a cause-effect relationship between news coverage and policy formation, the CNN effect may still be useful in considering media's constructivist shaping of an environment in which international relations and foreign policy may be formed, reconsidered, and challenged.[19]

Twitter and International Relations

Twenty years after the CNN effect, in which media became significant actors in foreign policy formation, we are once again experiencing a transformation of our media environment. This "information revolution" changes the character, structure, and accessibility of information as it disrupts the existing "information regime."[20] As the political establishment negotiate with these new media technologies, a new information regime is forged with unique informational properties that create opportunities and constraints for information management and in turn create different political structures.[21] These new political structures impact everything from domestic politics to international relations.

The defining transformation of today's emerging information and communication technologies (ICT) is their capacity for "scale shifting."[22] Scale shifting describes how "significant communicative acts with political and social effects *bypass states and traditional media alike*" (emphasis original).[23] Of these ICTs the rise of Twitter and other forms of social media have had the most visible power to transform "the character of our public discourse"[24] and collective activism.[25] Thus social media become a new focal point to understand political communication and international relations.

The burgeoning scholarship on social media politics focus on four dimensions: political establishment (e.g., parties, candidates), publics (e.g., everyday users, protesters, activists), journalism, and media events (e.g., campaigns).[26] Studies on the political establishment focus on their adoption and use of Twitter as well as their degree of influence. On the other hand, studies examining publics do so in terms of network structures and communication patterns while those on journalism look to understand how the fourth estate operates on Twitter. Finally, scholars examine tweets' prevalence and opinion expressions (of an admittedly limited public) related to media events.[27]

At the intersection of social media and IR even more remains under investigation and is just beginning to emerge. For those IR scholars who have recognized the importance of social media to their field, public or digital diplomacy—the use of digital communications for diplomatic purposes—has become the focal point of their research and "Twiplomacy,"[28] a subset of that research. As a nascent area of concern, most of these works focus on definitions, purposes, general evaluations, and proposed strategies for effective use of social media with domestic and foreign publics or foreign statesmen. We found a few case studies and content analyses covering the countries of Britain,[29] Haiti,[30] Japan,[31] Venezuela,[32] Iran.[33] However, these largely remained brief, descriptive introductions that stopped short of examining specific communicative practices and their capacity for changes in foreign policy. Khatib, Dutton, and Thelwall remains the exception with their in-depth case study on U.S. outreach to the Middle East.[34]

From the CNN effect to Twitter diplomacy, media have become major players in IR and deserve scholarly attention. As our Twitter-in-Chief, Trump provides ample opportunity to examine the role of Twitter in constructing an international reality and its affordances for shaping foreign policy. A close study of his tweets on China will add to the young and fragmented knowledge on social media IR by considering how Twitter, situated within a larger and complex media environment, mediates international relations and foreign policy. International relations are no longer the exclusive domain of statesmen but are also now the domain of media and publics. While some studies have examined institutionalized efforts of using social media for diplomacy, Trump's accidental diplomacy offers an opportunity to examine how a prominent businessman and then the president himself may use social media for diplomatic purposes. Furthermore, by engaging Trump's tweets on China, we expand the existing literature into the Asian context.

DISSECTING TRUMP'S TWEETS ON CHINA

This case study is to understand how Donald Trump, as a public figure, uses his social media presence to shape public understanding of other nations and potentially foreign policy. To achieve this research goal, we conducted a two-step case study, collecting data from both social and traditional media, subjected them both to content analysis and in-depth textual analysis.

Twitter

Trump's tweets were collected from Brendan Brown's Trump Twitter Archive, a database freely available via the web (http://www.trumptwitter archive.com/). The archive monitors Trump's primary account, @realDonald Trump, in real time as of January 27, 2017, and updated a few times a day before that point. Although the archive goes back as far as 2009, there are approximately four thousand tweets missing from the database. The Trump Twitter Archive remains one of the most comprehensive databases of Trump's tweets.

We used the U.S. Department of State's list of countries to search the archive and to determine the top ten countries in Trump's feed from 2009 to August 18, 2017. The top ten countries were as follows: China (433), Iran (254), Russia (200), Iraq (161), Mexico (136), Syria (131), Israel (116), Cuba (88), India (74), and Canada (60). Given the prevalence of Russia in the political discourse surrounding the 2016 election, these findings may be surprising. The following graph supports this impression as only Mexico ranked higher in number of tweets in 2016 and Russia has dominated Trump's Twitter feed of 2017 so far. However, the following graph (figure 4.1) also helps visualize Trump's long held concern of China, which spiked dramatically in the 2012 election and remains the second highest tweeted country of 2017 so far. By tracing tweets from beginning on China we can see his evolution from

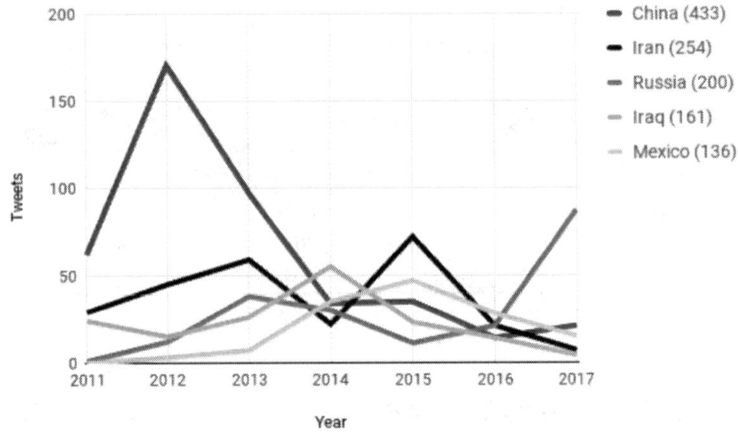

Figure 4.1.

the perspective of a prominent businessman to that of Republican candidate and finally president-elect and president.

Media Coverage

To see the interplay between social media and traditional media on international relations we also sought to collect traditional media coverage sparked by Trump's tweets on China. Unfortunately, collecting all the coverage for the span of six years (the first mention in the archive occurs in 2011) or even the entirety of the 2016 campaign was not feasible for this particular study. Therefore, we focused on the media event that surrounded Trump's tweet about his phone call with the president of Taiwan, a violation of the forty-year-old One China policy. This incident appeared to be Trump's first foreign policy move as president-elect.

We selected newspapers to represent traditional media because cable news often used them as sources and often commended them for their strong investigative journalism this election cycle. Based on a Pew research study on "Political Polarization & Media Habits," we selected newspapers based on reputation and where their primary audience falls on the political spectrum.[35] The *New York Times*, *Washington Post*, and *Boston Globe* were selected for left-of-center audiences, the *Los Angeles Times* for center, and the *Chicago Tribune* and *Wall Street Journal* for right-of-center audiences.

Each newspaper's website was used to retrieve the relevant articles where possible. For *Boston Globe*, which outsources to a clunky version of Google Search, and *Wall Street Journal*, which had a high pay wall, ProQuest was used instead. We used the search terms "Trump and Taiwan" and constrained the results to December 2, 2016, (the date of Trump's tweet) to December 16, 2016. These results were further filtered to exclude summaries and mere mentions of the incident. The articles that remained either mentioned Taiwan in the headline or lead of the story. The final count for analysis is as follows: *New York Times* (3), *Washington Post* (22), *Los Angeles Times* (16), *Chicago Tribune* (13), and *Wall Street Journal* (18).

Open Coding and In-depth Textual Analysis

We analyzed this data using both quantitative and qualitative methods. To gain an overall quantitative impression of the data, we first used Voyant, a web-based textual analysis software. Voyant provides word frequencies, chronological maps of word occurrences, and relationships between words. Next, we used open coding to qualitatively engage with the text and identify initial categories and patterns. According to Strauss and Corbin, open coding refers to "The analytical process through which concepts are identified and their properties and dimensions are discovered in data."[36] By doing so we established a codebook for the tweets to determine the frequency of their topics and rhetorical techniques. From these coded tweets we selected prime examples for in-depth analysis. Applying the same approach to the newspaper coverage, we searched for high-level concepts (i.e., thematic categories) and the editorial stance toward the incident caused by Trump's tweets (i.e., commendable, skirting support, mixed feelings, cautionary, critical, and neutral). The detailed description of our findings will be introduced in the next section.

CONSTRUCTING CHINA THROUGH TWITTER

Every communication channel shapes our perception of others. When the world is articulated through Twitter, a unique picture is constructed. What does that picture look like? How is it constructed? And what are the implications of its construction? Below we discuss our findings in three sections. The first section addresses the topical, rhetorical, and structural makeup of Trump's tweets on China whereas the second and third sections closely analyze their symbolic construction of China and assess their diplomatic potential.

Tweeting China

Media have associated any number of negative adjectives with Trump including childish,[37] angry,[38] and dark,[39] but Neal Gabler[40] describes Trump "as a man of his technological moment." According to Gabler, Trump's personality befits the medium and its underlying logic.[41] Both Trump's general communication style and Twitter's streamlined 140-character posts are defined by their simple, impulsive, and uncivil character.[42] We perform a topical, rhetorical, and structural analysis below to see if Trump's tweets on China follow such a construction.

The corpus of Trump tweets consists of 8,450 total words and 1,967 unique word forms, thus 77 percent are words you have read before. Reading through the corpus quickly becomes very repetitive. Of Trump's most frequently used words our search term "China" (and its variants: "China's" and "Chinese") came out on top by far with 507 counts. The second highest term at 129 counts was the "economy" (and its variants "economic," "economically," "economists," "jobs," "trade," "currency," and "money"). The economy was Trump's issue of choice when it came to China. Interestingly, the next highest term was tied to domestic politics, "barackobama" (and its variants: "Obama" and "Obama's") had 95 counts. These numbers help support Trump's propensity to use China as a means of attack against domestic leaders, especially Barack Obama. The fourth highest term also had little to do with China per se. America (and its variants: "Americans," "USA," "U.S.A.," "U.S.," and "country" as it applied to the United States) had 67 counts indicating Trump may be using China as a foil to define an American identity. Wrapping up the top five most frequent words comes a surprising term: "laughing" (and its variants: "laugh," "laughs," and "laughed"). Despite the positive connotations of the word itself, Trump invoked the term to establish an adversarial relationship between the United States and China—as if China is ridiculing the United States The impact of doing so turns China as an abstract concept into a personification that Trump and his followers could oppose.

A typical Trump tweet on China consists of a topic and a rhetorical construction. Using open coding we identified ten topics and ten rhetorical techniques among the 433 tweets on China. Topics include: trade/economy (202), domestic politics (197), international affairs[43] (109), military/national security (104), oil/energy (49), debt (40), environment (13), humanitarian (11), infrastructure (8), health (5), and immigration (3). Meanwhile rhetorical constructions consist of the following categories and operational definitions:

- issue statement—expression of fact-like information[44] (135)
- self-promotion/self-congratulatory—expression of Trump achievement (81)
- humor—expression with a comic effect (15)
- praise—expression commending a person, party, or entity (25)
- domestic leadership criticism—expression condemning U.S. leaders by name or institution title (137)
- international leadership criticism—expression condemning international leadership (not necessarily by name) (25)
- competition/enemy construction—expression situating an actor as competitor or enemy (277)

- foreboding/doomsday—expression predicting crisis or great danger (46)
- emotional venting—expression quickly releasing emotion (53)
- other—expression not categorized above (9)

Each tweet may refer to more than one topic and may invoke more than one rhetorical construction. For instance, the following tweet was coded for its topic, trade/economy, and rhetorical construction, issue statement, and competition.

> Wow, China exports rise 15% in September. They are laughing at USA![45]

Defined by their topics and rhetorical constructions, Trump's China tweets typically also follow one of three structures. The first is a straightforward, seemingly objective presentation of an event. For example,

> Hillary Clinton surged the trade deficit with China 40% as Secretary of State, costing Americans millions of jobs.[46]

The second consists of two subtypes: one that pairs a seemingly objective presentation with an interpretation and one that pairs a seemingly objective presentation with a call to action. For example, Trump provides his interpretation of Beijing's decision to add taxes on United States auto exports in 2011. Rather than depicting a descriptive cause and effect (e.g., this tariff will hurt the U.S. auto industry) he frames the situation and its interpretation for his followers.

> China just put a tariff on US cars and trucks—22%—China is laughing at our inept leaders. @BarackObama[47]

In the following tweet, Trump provides a call to action—a suggestion for a retaliatory tariff on Chinese goods entering the U.S. This suggestion is clearly actionable (even with its question construction) rather than merely interpretive.

> China taxing imports from the US—22%—why aren't we taxing China?[48]

The final structure abandons the seemingly objective presentation for an exclusively interpretive or actionable message. For instance, without providing any context or evidence, the interpretive tweet below invoked a humor rhetorical construction to criticize Obama's gullibility and compliance with China.

> Have you heard? China just told Obama to jump. Obama asked how high.[49]

Overall, the first look at Trump's tweets on China revealed a similar communicative pattern on this microblogging platform than previously reported.[50]

We found his tweets to be simple, repetitious, and prone to emotional outbursts. The vocabulary was straightforward and unpretentious. Exceptions, such as his tweet regarding China's challenge to the U.S.'s "economic hegemony," notably stood out from the overall corpus.[51] Trump's tweets also take on an emotional character. He occasionally employed all caps (19), frequently implemented exclamation marks (129 counts), and had at least 53 counts of particularly strong outbursts of emotion, which we classified as emotional venting (e.g., "SAD!"). He's driven by a narrow set of topics that appeal to his sensibility as a businessman (trade/economy, oil/energy, debt, etc.).[52] Using an economic lens toward China enables great opportunities to present a competition framework often found in the realm of business. Some of Trump's tweets on China provide additional examples of his widely reported uncivil discourse; however, that incivility is mostly directed at domestic foes (e.g., "Crooked Hillary," "Lightweight @DannyZuker is too stupid," "@KarlRove is a biased dope," "Our leaders are so stupid!").[53]

FRAMING CHINA IN 140 CHARACTERS

Twitter's 140 characters may truncate the expression of ideas, but it does not diminish the capacity of language to construct reality. Closely reading Trump's tweets evokes specific images of China, images of a rival, a nemesis, a weapon, and an irresponsible leader. These images reinforce the long-existing adversarial U.S.-China relationship and lays the groundwork for general policy responses that ignore the cooperative relationship between the two nations since the late 1970s.

Rivalry Frame

During his six years tweeting about China, Trump's most common and most consistent frame is that of the rival. This frame has been used to discuss diverse topics, such as trade/economy, oil/energy, military/national security, and infrastructure, from an economic perspective. In Trump's definition, China is more like a rival company in the global economic arena than a political entity. As such, he adopts a relentless zero-sum mentality to interpret China's international dealings. A win for China equals a loss for the United States In one example, Trump laments the initial U.S. rejection of the Keystone pipeline, which resulted in Canada selling their oil to China. He labeled China's $1.5 billion oil deal as "A terrible deal for US!"[54] This rivalry is further complicated by Trump's accusations of China's unfair tactics (e.g., currency manipulation, deceitful maneuvers). However, Trump is not casting a moral judgment on what he perceives to be the Chinese approach to all their international dealings. Instead, he admires their ingenuity and he bemoans the United States' inability to use those same strategies.

> Remember, we don't get any oil from Iraq, China gets whatever ISIS hasn't already taken. So why isn't China sending the troops? Too smart![55]

These rare moments of praise stand out as dramatic shifts in tone from Trump's general negativity toward China. He considers them to be smart in their dealings—spending and exerting the least amount of resources for the most profit—a genuinely bottom-line driven approach to international relations. Consequently, the rivalry frame oversimplifies international relations as a zero-sum game in which there can be no compromising or cooperation. This antagonistic zero-sum mentality reinforces a common perspective in U.S.-China relations,[56] which Harry Harding[57] reports has led some to refer to these relations as the "New Cold War."

Nemesis Frame

Seeing the economy as the lifeblood of a nation's survival, Trump's rival frame often escalates into the nemesis frame in which China is constructed as an enemy threatening U.S. sovereignty. This frame is evident in Trump's recurring discussion of currency manipulation (an inaccurate and outdated issue):

> China's currency manipulation is one of our nation's greatest sovereign threats. The yuan has appreciated 40% against our dollar since 2005[58]

> China is not our friend. They are not our ally. They want to overtake us, and if we don't get smart and tough soon, they will.[59]

The nemesis frame goes beyond the economic realm to accuse China of engaging in military and government espionage, or tying China with other foreign foes (e.g., Iran). However, the aim of this frame appears to be less about demonizing China than fostering domestic solidarity. Using this nemesis frame, Trump presents a unifying threat against which we the people must protect our economic system and in turn, our way of life.

Weapon Frame

Capitalizing on the opposition of the rival and the nemesis frames, Trump often wields China as a token to attack domestic foes. He wields this weapon in one of three ways. The first is to use China as a barometer against which to measure domestic foes' capacity for international relations competence. For example,

> Lightweight @DannyZuker is too stupid to see that China (and others) is destroying the U.S. economically and our leaders are helpless! SAD.[60]

In this case, Danny Zuker, an American television writer and producer, exemplifies in Trump's view a poor understanding of China, which Trump uses as grounds for attack. The second is to use a domestic issue as a way of forecasting the actor's capacity to deal with China.

> If Crooked Hillary Clinton can't close the deal on Crazy Bernie, how is she going to take on China, Russia, ISIS and all of the others?[61]

Because Trump uses China as the ultimate challenge, perceived weaknesses on other issues become grounds to question that actor's competence to take on U.S.-China relations. No matter an actor's understanding of China or actual relations with China, Trump often attacks domestic foes, especially Barack Obama, by insinuating good relations with China.

> It's Thursday and only 26 days until the election. How many illegal donations from China and Saudi Arabia did Obama collect today?[62]

The purpose of the weapon frame is to critique domestic foes to score political points and to evidence his superior leadership ability. In other words, to paint himself as a leader with the knowledge, necessary animosity, and the daring to deal with China.

Irresponsible Leader Frame

The evolution of Trump's tweets, especially post presidency, indicates a transformation of perspective as Trump began to see China less as a rival company and more as a political entity who needs to share international responsibility. The irresponsible leader frame thus works as a call to action for China through complaints, bargaining, and praise. For instance, facing the most recent North Korea nuclear crisis, Trump first complained about China's indifference, which he deemed all the more striking after years of China benefiting from the U.S. economy:

> China has been taking out massive amounts of money & wealth from the U.S. in totally one-sided trade, but won't help with North Korea. Nice![63]

His frustration then turned into bargaining both hard and soft. In one tweet, Trump made it clear that a better trade deal would only be possible if China would help mediate the North Korea situation. Five days later, Trump implied he would quit calling China a "currency manipulator" if they worked with the United States on the North Korea problem.[64] Twelve days later, he tried yet another strategy, this time praise.

> North Korea disrespected the wishes of China & its highly respected President when it launched, though unsuccessfully, a missile today. Bad![65]

Although communicated as praise, the implication of this tweet is that China is unable to control its unruly neighbor, and needs to make a more concerted effort to do so. Regardless of the frame's style, Trump constructs a China that failed its responsibility to lead on the world stage, and thus he echoes former deputy secretary of state Robert Zoellick's 2005 "responsible stakeholder" rebuke of China.[66]

THE FOURTH ESTATE TAKES ON TRUMP AND CHINA

While Trump's tweets became frequent fodder for election coverage, his tweets on China received increased media attention once Trump was in a position to actually affect foreign policy. The most notable example of such media engagement took place just shy of one month after the election as President-Elect Trump tweeted about his call with Taiwan. On December 2, 2016, Trump tweeted: "The President of Taiwan CALLED ME today to wish me congratulations on winning the Presidency. Thank you!"[67] Controversy swarmed as this tweet effectively ended the forty-year presidential protocol of acknowledging the "One China" policy. One hour later, Trump apparently responding to the criticism continued: "Interesting how the U.S. sells Taiwan billions of dollars of military equipment but I should not accept a congratulatory call."[68] Trump added fuel to the fire two days later by directly criticizing China (and indirectly the foreign policy establishment) for the double standard it applied to the United States: "Did China ask us if it was OK to devalue their currency (making it hard for our companies to compete), heavily tax our products going into . . . their country (the U.S. doesn't tax them) or to build a massive military complex in the middle of the South China Sea? I don't think so!"[69] For the following two weeks, media debated these tweets for their foreign policy implications.

Although they do so to varying degrees, most of the articles (which included news, commentaries, opinions, and editorials) sought to explain the

"One China" policy and why China and foreign policy experts considered Trump's call to be a violation. The *New York Times* and *Washington Post* both had lengthy informational pieces providing the deeper historical context for the policy as well as for U.S.-China and China-Taiwan relations. They note the origin of the policy (1972, 1979 Nixon administration), the purpose in U.S. terms (to not anger the growing military and economic power of China and to reinforce trading partnership with China), and the unofficial arrangement with Taiwan (earlier as a military base and later as a trading partner and as a fledgling democracy). Some opinion pieces in the *Los Angeles Times* and *Chicago Tribune* provided such coverage as well. Providing this backdrop served as the foundation for their framing of the event. It was Trump's violation that made the "One China" policy news, but it was the violation and what it indicated about Trump's leadership abilities that became the story.

Given the uncertainty of Trump's intentions, debating Trump's competence was most prevalent among such discussions. Journalists aimed to understand the character of the incident—a misstep or a deliberate shift in policy—and framed Trump as either the *ignorant outsider*, the *resolute leader*, or the *madman*.[70]

The ignorant outsider frame depicted Trump as unaware of the "One China" policy and oblivious to its meaning for diplomatic protocol and its impact on U.S.-China relations. The ignorant outsider frame was prevalent in articles that were either critical or cautionary about Trump's actions in the Taiwan incident. In an op-ed entitled "Trump's stumbling first steps on the world stage," the *Los Angeles Times* editorial board demonstrated the strongest and clearest instance of this frame.[71] The editorial board framed Trump as "unschooled"[72] on matters of foreign policy and his approach as "stumbling,"[73] "blundering,"[74] and "impulsive."[75] They argued that his ignorance led to "a month of misfires and missed opportunities" that would be sure to worsen if he continued to refuse his intelligence briefings, an often reported account in articles adopting this frame.[76] For instance, Jennifer Rubin's "Trump's Taiwan charade" in the *Washington Post*, argues Trump was either ignorant of the policy, ignorant of the significance of the call, or ignorant of the reception the violation would produce.[77] In any case, she concludes that Trump "cannot get an experienced secretary of state pick in there fast enough to exercise some adult supervision."[78] The ignorance frame was less about the learning curve that all incoming presidents face or even Trump's steep learning curve as an outsider of the political arena, and more about the dangers that would befall the United States specifically because of Trump's perceived lackadaisical approach to foreign policy.

In direct opposition to this understanding of the event is the resolute leader frame. Here Trump's actions are viewed as an intentional, commendable, and even clever shakeup of an outdated policy and relationship (U.S.-China, U.S.-Taiwan) in need of revision. Marc A. Thiessen crafts such a frame for both the *Washington Post* ("Trump's Taiwan call wasn't a blunder. It was brilliant") and the *Chicago Tribune* ("Trump's brilliant Taiwan move: The right message to send").[79] He is confident that Trump made a calculated move—first with his call and then through his tweets—to communicate his independence from prior policies and general diplomatic conventions. Instead of comparing Trump's actions to diplomatic precedent, these authors often note the internal coherence of this specific incident with Trump's previous discourse, for example, his 2011 tweets looking to get tough on China by increasing relations (the sale of F-16s) to Taiwan.[80] Authors adopting this frame consider Trump's actions necessary and potentially effective. For instance, Rupert Hammond-Chambers of the *Wall Street Journal* ("America's Dangerous Drift on Taiwan") concludes the Chinese are essentially rational agents driven by their own self-interests, which ultimately depends on a productive relationship with the United States.[81] And according to Thiessen, Trump has given himself an opportunity Obama did not, that is to improve U.S.-China relations while simultaneously growing the U.S.-Taiwan trade partnership.[82] Praise for Trump was often paired with criticism for Obama, from general critiques of Obama's "lethargic" and overly cautious approach to foreign policy to the specific hypocrisy of Obama's well received outreach to Cuba.[83] The resolute leader frame looks to advocate a new perspective on the U.S.-China relationship and provide a sense of reassurance, especially in light of what they deem to be media's "19th nervous breakdown."[84]

Most authors presenting a strong and clear frame opted for the ignorant outsider or the resolute leader, but the madman frame appeared in a handful of articles. This frame is less about the "One China" policy and more about the need for caution as Trump endeavors to be unpredictable in all foreign relations. The sentiments of authors using this frame range greatly. Mild critiques simply frame Trump as unpredictable, such as the *Los Angeles Times*'s "Trump's unpredictability is likely to unnerve both allies and adversaries."[85] Stronger rebukes evoke images of chaos, such as the all popular "Tweet storm"[86] or "Twitter storm"[87] found in the *Washington Post*. David Ignatius ("Trump flunks his first foreign policy test") goes so far as to refer to Trump as "an American Kim Jong Un," and thus truly evoking the imagery of a madman.[88] During the campaign, "the sense that Trump would do, say or tweet anything helped him immensely, diverting from controversies and persuading voters that he would set Washington ablaze."[89] However, as president-elect and president, these authors worry about both the frequency and severity of diplomatic crises Trump will face if he continues to utilize the same strategies. The aim of this frame is to use the Taiwan incident to encourage Trump to be more cautious or even to abandon his tactics now that he has achieved the presidency. As Ignatius of the *Washington Post* concludes, "Let's hope he learns something."[90]

Through their definitions of the "One China" policy, these traditional media demonstrated their capacity for lengthier contextual examinations and the valuable role they continue to serve in the age of Twitter. Understanding precedent and historical relationships is foundational to foreign policy debates and these media provide readers with some background to evaluate Trump's actions. These media outlets engaged in such evaluations as well; however, these evaluations eschewed the policy itself in favor of the violation and Trump's leadership. Only three articles, all in the *Washington Post*, questioned the morality of the "One China" policy itself, and they did so from the Taiwanese perspective. Lin Fei-fan, Chen Wei-ting, and June Lin, three Taiwanese social activists ("Americans should stop using Taiwan to score political points against Trump and China"), and Shawna Yang Ryan, a Taiwanese American writer and professor ("Taiwan is a country with history and people. It's not just a diplomatic nuisance"), penned articles critical of the media and foreign policy establishment for failing to reconsider an outdated policy and framing the story only via Beijing terms.[91] The third, by the American journalist John Pomfret ("America's overreaction to Trump's Taiwan call is dangerous"), worries for Taiwan and urges Trump to protect Taiwan on the moral grounds of securing democracy.[92] While these three authors come to Taiwan's defense, Taiwan in and of itself is largely neglected by other media and foreign policy responses. The absence impedes productive foreign policy debate.

WHEN FOREIGN POLICY MEETS TWITTER: THE BIRTH OF A NEW INTERNATIONAL REALITY

Despite facing heavy criticism from all parties, President Trump continues to use Twitter—his preferred means of communication—to air his unfiltered thoughts on foreign issues. Because of their sheer number (433) and diversity (e.g., topical and rhetorical constructions), his tweets on China over the span of six years (2011–2017) provide a rich source for us to examine the intersection between social media and international relations as well as the co-constitutive relations between social media and traditional media on debating foreign policy.

Using both quantitative and qualitative methods to closely read these tweets, we found Trump painted a specific image of China for his followers. As our findings suggest, Trump's tweets on China organized themselves in a repetitious structure laden with negative sentiments. These tweets often read as emotional outbursts at best, but more often, they functioned as political attacks on either China or Trump's domestic foes. Driven mostly by economic concerns and a competition framework, these tweets construct China as a rivalry company in the global economic arena whose competitiveness quickly becomes a threat to the sovereignty and national security of the United States Framing China as a rival and an enemy thus grants Trump legitimacy to question his domestic foes' capacity to handle issues on China, which he constructs as the ultimate challenge for any leader engaged in international relations. Meanwhile, Trump also used the irresponsible leader frame to accuse China of evading its responsibility on international affairs. Together, these tweets reveal Trump's adversarial perspective on China and explain his abrupt departure from the long acknowledged One China policy.

The series of now famous Taiwan phone call tweets thus demonstrate Twitter's potential impact on foreign policy formation or negotiation. Shocked by the explicit protocol violation, traditional media swarmed into the diplomatic battleground. More than merely gauging the meaning of the president's tweets, their coverage evaluated the diplomatic appropriateness of Trump's actions—taking the phone call and making it public on social media. Journalists framed Trump either as an ignorant outsider who is inexperienced in dealing with foreign issues, a resolute leader who gave China a clever punch, or a madman who tried to score political points with his unpredictability. Consequently, the media's (over)reaction toward this incident reveal a new international reality in which Twitter, with its real-time interactivity and global reach, has become an instrument of foreign policy.

How might Twitter, as a new form of communication technology and a new mode of communication, shape the public's perception on foreign affairs and further influence policy formation? We suggest three possible transformations. First, the structural logic of Twitter forces a simplification of international affairs. Given its 140-character limitation, Twitter is not an ideal platform for sophisticated debate. Twitter users are trained to reduce the details of their messages to craft a catchy soundbite with personality. They tend to use links or videos as supplements to enhance their tweet if necessary. According to Ott, "[O]ne can philosophize *about* Twitter but not *on* Twitter."[93] The intervention of Twitter thus exacerbates a shallow and reductive public perception of international affairs in which the historical context is erased and the morality of foreign policies is overlooked.

Secondly, the affective dimensions of Twitter encourage more isolationist and protectionist approaches to international affairs. Studies have shown that "emotionally charged Twitter messages tend to be retweeted more often and more quickly compared to neutral ones."[94] As such, discourses dominated by populist sentiments have the most potential to go viral on Twitter because they are laden with strong emotions defined by narrow nationalism. This would redraw the line between "us" and "them" and see the foreign countries as either our friends or foes. With the help of hashtags, both narratives can go viral in Trump's Twitterville.

Thirdly, the legitimization of Twitter by mainstream media would make it an instrument for world leaders to wage a mediated "asymmetric war" on other countries.[95] According to Gilsinan and Friedman, asymmetric war refers to widespread guerrilla tactics "to spread out the 'adversary's' resources and prevent them from concentrating enough force in any one place to produce a decisive outcome."[96] As seen in the case of Trump, tweets have become official statements published and discussed by mainstream media. The intense news coverage not only helped to distribute "misinformation," but also spur a swarm of international concern and attention trying to understand the meaning behind those microblogging messages. Twitter and the associated media attention thus can be used as tactics for weaker countries to create shock, distraction, and confusion to erode and exhaust their opponents in a stronger position.

Only time will tell how the relations between Twitter and foreign policy will develop. While some foreign leaders follow Trump's lead to exchange their personal thoughts on Twitter, such as Israeli prime minister Benjamin Netanyahu, other countries like China and North Korea block a variety of social media platforms, including Twitter. Such nations, nevertheless, often engage with Trump's tweets through more traditional media. One thing for sure is that this new form of communication has begun to have real consequences in international politics.

NOTES

1. Robert F. Kennedy, *Thirteen Days: A Memoir of the Cuban Missile Crisis* (New York: W. W. Norton & Company, 1971/1999).
2. Donald J. Trump. Twitter post, July 8, 2017, 1:55 p.m., https://twitter.com/realdonaldtrump/status/883761448064864257.
3. Donald J. Trump. July 29, 2017, 6:29 p.m., https://twitter.com/realdonaldtrump/status/891440474132795392.
4. Ben Westcott, "Chinese Media to Trump: Stop the 'Emotional Venting' on Twitter," *CNN* (Atlanta, GA), Aug. 2, 2017.
5. W. Joseph Campbell, *Yellow Journalism: Puncturing the Myths, Defining the Legacies* (Westport, CT: Praeger Publishers, 2001).
6. Piers Robinson, "The CNN Effect Reconsidered: Mapping a Research Agenda for the Future," *Media, War & Conflict* 4, no. 1 (2011): 3–11.

7. Filiz Coban, "The Role of the Media in International Relations: From the CNN Effect to the Al-Jazeere Effect," *Journal of International Relations and Foreign Policy* 4, no. 2 (2016): 46; David Shambaugh, "Tangled Titans: Conceptualizing the U.S.-China Relationship," in *Tangled Titans: The United States and China* 2013, ed. David Shambaugh (Lanham, MD: Rowman & Littlefield Publishers, 2013), 3–26.

8. Filiz Coban, "The Role of the Media in International Relations: From the CNN Effect to the Al-Jazeere Effect," *Journal of International Relations and Foreign Policy* 4, no. 2 (2016): 46; Piers Robinson, "The CNN Effect Reconsidered: Mapping a Research Agenda for the Future," *Media, War & Conflict* 4, no. 1 (2011): 4.

9. David Shambaugh, "Tangled Titans: Conceptualizing the U.S.-China Relationship," in *Tangled Titans: The United States and China* 2013, ed. David Shambaugh (Lanham, MD: Rowman & Littlefield Publishers, 2013), 14.

10. Piers Robinson, "The CNN Effect Reconsidered: Mapping a Research Agenda for the Future," *Media, War & Conflict* 4, no. 1 (2011): 4.

11. David Shambaugh, "Tangled Titans: Conceptualizing the U.S.-China Relationship," in *Tangled Titans: The United States and China* 2013, ed. David Shambaugh (Lanham, MD: Rowman & Littlefield Publishers, 2013), 18.

12. Piers Robinson, "The CNN Effect Reconsidered: Mapping a Research Agenda for the Future," *Media, War & Conflict* 4, no. 1 (2011): 5.

13. Steven Livingston, *Clarifying the CNN Effect: An Examination of Media Effects According to Type of Military Intervention* (Cambridge, MA: The John Shorenstein Barone Center on the Press, Politics, and Public Policy at Harvard University, 1997); Piers Robinson, "The CNN Effect Revisited," *Critical Studies in Media Communication* 22, no. 4 (2005): 344–349.

14. Eytan Gilboa, "The CNN Effect: The Search for a Communication Theory of International Relations." *Political Communication* 22 (2005): 27–44.

15. Ibid.; Steven Livingston, "The CNN Effect Reconsidered (Again): Problematizing ICT and Global Governance in the CNN Effect Research Agenda," *Media, War & Conflict* 4, no. 1 (2011): 20–36; Piers Robinson, "The CNN Effect Reconsidered: Mapping a Research Agenda for the Future," *Media, War & Conflict* 4, no. 1 (2011).

16. Philip Seib, *The Global Journalists: News and Conscience in a World of Conflict* (Lanham, MD: Rowman & Littlefield, 2002), 27.

17. Steven Livingston, *Clarifying the CNN Effect: An Examination of Media Effects According to Type of Military Intervention* (Cambridge, MA: The John Shorenstein Barone Center on the Press, Politics, and Public Policy at Harvard University, 1997), 2–10.

18. Peter Jakobsen, "Focus on the CNN Effect Misses the Points: What Triggers UN Peace Enforcement after the Cold War?" *Journal of Peace Research*, no. 33 (2000): 131–143; Philip Seib, *The Global Journalists: News and Conscience in a World of Conflict* (Lanham, MD: Rowman & Littlefield, 2002), 27.

19. Timothy McNulty, "Television's Impact on Executive Decision Making and Diplomacy," *Fletcher Forum of World Affairs*, no. 17 (1993): 67–83.

20. Bruce Bimber, *Information and American Democracy: Technology in the Evolution of Political Power* (Cambridge, UK: Cambridge University Press, 2003), 18.

21. Ibid.

22. Sidney Tarrow, *The New Transnational Activism* (Cambridge, UK: Cambridge University Press, 2005), 120.

23. Steven Livingston, *Clarifying the CNN Effect: An Examination of Media Effects According to Type of Military Intervention* (Cambridge, MA: The John Shorenstein Barone Center on the Press, Politics, and Public Policy at Harvard University, 1997), 28.

24. Brian L. Ott, "The Age of Twitter: Donald J. Trump and the Politics of Debasement," *Critical Studies in Media Communication* 34, no. 1 (2017): 59.

25. W. Lance Bennett and Alexandra Segerberg, "The Logic of Connective Action: Digital Media and the Personalization of Contentious Politics," *Information, Communication & Society* 15, no. 5 (2012): 739–768.

26. Andreas Jungherr, "Twitter Use in Election Campaigns: A Systematic Literature Review," *Journal of Information Technology & Politics* 13, no. 1 (2016): 72–91.

27. Ibid.

28. Matthias Lüfkens, "Twiplomacy Study 2012," *Twiplomacy*, June 25, 2012, http://twiplomacy.com/blog/twiplomacy-study-2012/.

29. Simon Usherwood and Katharine A. M. Wright, "Sticks and Stones: Comparing Twitter Campaigning Strategies in the EU Referendum," *The British Journal of Politics and International Relations*, 19, no. 2 (2017): 371–388.

30. Britney Harris, "Diplomacy 2.0: The Future of Social Media in Nation Branding," *Exchange: The Journal of Public Diplomacy* 4, no. 1 (2013):17–32.

31. Ibid.

32. Ibid.; Craig Hayden, "Engaging Technologies: A Comparative Study of U.S. and Venezuelan Strategies of Influence and Public Diplomacy," *International Journal of Communication*, no. 7 (2013): 1–25.

33. Constance Duncombe, "Twitter and Transformative Diplomacy: Social Media and Iran-US Relations," *International Affairs* 93, no. 3 (2017): 545–562.

34. Lina Khatib, William Dutton, and Michael Thelwall, "Public Diplomacy 2.0: A Case Study of the US Digital Outreach Team," *Middle East Journal* 66, no. 3 (2012): 453–472.

35. Amy Mitchell, Jeffrey Gottfried, Jocelyn Kiley, and Katerina Eva Matsa, "Political Polarization & Media Habits," *Pew Research Center*, October 21, 2014, http://www.journalism.org/2014/10/21/political-polarization-media-habits/.

36. Anselm Strauss and Juliet Corbin, *Basics of Qualitative Research: Techniques and Procedures for Developing Grounded Theory* (London, UK: Sage, 1998), 101.

37. Kathleen Parker, "Trump's Two-Year Presidency," *Washington Post* (Washington, DC), Feb. 10, 2017.

38. Mark Landler and Maggie Haberman, "Angry Trump Grilled His Generals about Troop Increase, Then Gave In," *New York Times* (New York, NY), Aug. 21, 2017.

39. Aaron Bandler, "There's One Word the Entire Media Used to Describe Trump Last Night. Guess What It Is," *Dailywire*, July 22, 2016, http://www.dailywire.com/news/7734/theres-one-word-entire-media-used-describe-trump-aaron-bandler#exit-modal.

40. Neal Gabler, "Donald Trump, the Emperor of Social Media," *Moyers & Company*, April 29, 2016, http://billmoyers.com/story/donald-trump-the-emperor-of-social-media/, para. 2.

41. Neal Gabler, "Donald Trump, the Emperor of Social Media," Moyers & Company, April 29, 2016, http://billmoyers.com/story/donald-trump-the-emperor-of-social-media/.

42. Brian L. Ott, "The Age of Twitter: Donald J. Trump and the Politics of Debasement," *Critical Studies in Media Communication* 34, no. 1 (2017): 59.

43. Tweets were categorized as international affairs when it involved China and at least one other foreign country.

44. Tweets were categorized as issue statements only when Trump provided some semblance of factual evidence, i.e., statistics or external links to news articles. However, we did not examine the factuality or appropriateness of the information he supplied. Our focus here was how Trump constructed a sense of neutrality or objectivity for his message.

45. Donald J. Trump. Twitter post, October 13, 2014, 8:21 a.m., https://twitter.com/realdonaldtrump/status/521651877352857600.

46. Donald J. Trump. Twitter post, June 21, 2016, 11:38 a.m., https://twitter.com/realdonaldtrump/status/745294739092684800.

47. Donald J. Trump. Twitter post, December 16, 2011, 2:36 p.m., https://twitter.com/realdonaldtrump/status/147777192439459840.

48. Donald J. Trump. Twitter post, December 20, 2011, 9:04 a.m., https://twitter.com/realdonaldtrump/status/149143097090113537.

49. Donald J. Trump. Twitter post, October 3, 2012, 3:10 p.m., https://twitter.com/realdonaldtrump/status/253587791454294017.

50. Zachary Crockett, "What I Learned Analyzing 7 Months of Donald Trump's Tweets," *Vox*, May 16, 2016, https://www.vox.com/2016/5/16/11603854/donald-trump-twitter.

51. Donald J. Trump. Twitter post, August 7, 2012, 1:56 p.m., https://twitter.com/realdonaldtrump/status/232913045637189632.

52. Military/national security was the third most frequently mentioned topic. Given the prevalence of framing China in military terms during the 2012 Presidential run, we speculate Trump's endorsement of Mitt Romney and his "military-first" stance (Shambaugh, August 3, 2012, para. 4) may have contributed to Trump's increased implementation of the military frame.

53. Donald J. Trump. Twitter post, May 20, 2016, 4:47 a.m., https://twitter.com/realdonaldtrump/status/733594906447372292; Ibid., June 12, 2013, (8:25 p.m.), https://twitter.com/realdonaldtrump/status/344988801850015744; Ibid., November 12, 2015, (10:00 a.m.), https://twitter.com/realdonaldtrump/status/664820082325893121; Ibid., July 23, 2013, (6:29 a.m.)., https://twitter.com/realdonaldtrump/status/359636340666675200.

54. Donald J. Trump. Twitter post. July 31, 2012, 9:32 a.m., https://twitter.com/realdonaldtrump/status/230310078568345600.

55. Donald J. Trump. Twitter post, November 9, 2014, 3:08 a.m., https://twitter.com/realdonaldtrump/status/531372695917957120.

56. Rosemary Foot, "U.S.-China Interactions in Global Governance and International Organizations," in *Tangled Titans: The United States and China* 2013, ed. David Shambaugh (Lanham, MD: Rowman & Littlefield Publishers, 2013), 347–368.

57. Harry Harding, "American Visions of the Future of U.S.-China Relations: Competition, Cooperation, and Conflict," in *Tangled Titans: The United States and China* 2013, ed. David Shambaugh (Lanham, MD: Rowman & Littlefield Publishers, 2013), 389–409.

58. Donald J. Trump. Twitter post, June 13, 2012, 2:32 p.m., https://twitter.com/realdonaldtrump/status/212990869211578368.

59. Donald J. Trump. Twitter post, February 21, 2013, 2:35 p.m., https://twitter.com/realdonaldtrump/status/304690887248707584.

60. Donald J. Trump. Twitter post, June 12, 2013, 8:25 p.m., https://twitter.com/realdonaldtrump/status/344988801850015744.

61. Donald J. Trump. Twitter post, May 13, 2016, 8:03 p.m., https://twitter.com/realdonaldtrump/status/731288678451019776.

62. Donald J. Trump. Twitter post, October 11, 2012, 3:07 p.m., https://twitter.com/realdonaldtrump/status/256486209034022914.

63. Donald J. Trump. Twitter post, January 2, 2017, 5:47 p.m., https://twitter.com/realdonaldtrump/status/816068355555815424.

64. Donald J. Trump. Twitter post, April 16, 2017, 7:18 a.m., https://twitter.com/realdonaldtrump/status/853583417916755968.

65. Donald J. Trump. Twitter post, April 28, 2017, 6:26 p.m., https://twitter.com/realdonaldtrump/status/858100088253669376.

66. Robert B. Zoellick, "Whither China: From Membership to Responsibility?" U.S. Department of State Archive, September 21, 2005, https://2001–2009.state.gov/s/d/former/zoellick/rem/53682.htm, ¶. 9.

67. Donald J. Trump. Twitter post, December 2, 2016, 6:44 p.m., https://twitter.com/realdonaldtrump/status/804848711599882240.

68. Donald J. Trump. Twitter post, December 2, 2016, 7:41 p.m., https://twitter.com/realdonaldtrump/status/804863098138005504.

69. Donald J. Trump. Twitter post, December 4, 2016, 4:23 p.m., https://twitter.com/realdonaldtrump/status/805538149157969924.

70. A fourth frame was mentioned by a few authors, namely the gullible puppet—that Trump was being duped by advisors into defying the "One China" policy and challenging China. However, none of these authors clearly adopted this frame so it was not included in our discussion here.

71. *Times* Editorial Board, "Trump's Stumbling First Steps on the World Stage," *Los Angeles Times* (Los Angeles, CA), Dec. 7, 2016.

72. Ibid., para. 5.

73. Ibid., para. 2.

74. Ibid., para. 3.

75. Ibid., para. 10.

76. Ibid., para. 6.

77. Jennifer Rubin, "Trump's Taiwan Charade," *Washington Post* (Washington, DC), Dec. 4, 2016.

78. Ibid., para. 8.

79. Marc A. Thiessen, "Trump's Taiwan Call Wasn't a Blunder. It Was Brilliant," *Washington Post* (Washington, DC), Dec. 5, 2016; Marc A. Thiessen, "Trump's Bril-

liant Taiwan Move: The Right Message to Send," *Chicago Tribune* (Chicago, IL), Dec. 6, 2016.

80. Donald J. Trump. Twitter post, October 18, 2011, 9:16 a.m., https://twitter.com/realdonaldtrump/status/126300698945134593; Ibid., November 18, 2011, 2:34 p.m., https://twitter.com/realdonaldtrump/status/137629814998835200.

81. Rupert Hammond-Chambers, "America's Dangerous Drift on Taiwan," *Wall Street Journal* (New York, NY), Dec. 5, 2016.

82. Marc A. Thiessen, "Trump's Brilliant Taiwan Move: The Right Message to Send," *Chicago Tribune* (Chicago, IL), Dec. 6, 2016.

83. Ed Rogers, "Trump Is a Bold Antidote to the Lethargic Obama Years," *Chicago Tribune* (Chicago, IL), Dec. 8, 2016; Marc A. Thiessen, "Trump's Taiwan Call Wasn't a Blunder. It was Brilliant," *Washington Post* (Washington, DC), Dec. 5, 2016.

84. "Trump's Taiwan Play," *Wall Street Journal* (New York, NY), Dec. 5, 2016, para. 2.

85. Tribune News Services, "By Accident or Design, Trump Signals Tougher China Policy," *Los Angeles Times* (Los Angeles, CA), Dec. 5, 2016, para. 6.

86. Jennifer Rubin, "Trump's Taiwan Charade," *Washington Post* (Washington, DC), Dec. 4, 2016, para. 7.

87. David Ignatius, "Trump Flunks His First Foreign Policy Test," *Washington Post* (Washington, DC), Dec. 6, 2016, para. 5.

88. Ibid., para. 6.

89. Noah Bierman, "Trump Delivering on His Promise to Be Unpredictable on Foreign Affairs. Not Everyone's Convinced That's a Good Idea," *Los Angeles Times* (Los Angeles, CA), Dec. 16, 2016, para. 14.

90. David Ignatius, "Trump Flunks His First Foreign Policy Test," *Washington Post* (Washington, DC), Dec. 6, 2016, para. 15.

91. Lin Fei-fan, Chen Wei-ting, and June Lin, "Americans Should Stop Using Taiwan to Score Political Points against Trump and China," *Washington Post* (Washington, DC), Dec. 7, 2016; Shawna Yang Ryan, "Taiwan Is a Country with History and People. It's Not Just a Diplomatic Nuisance," *Washington Post* (Washington, DC), Dec. 9, 2016.

92. John Pomfret, "America's Overreaction to Trump's Taiwan Call Is Dangerous," *Washington Post* (Washington, DC), Dec. 9, 2016.

93. Brian L. Ott, "The Age of Twitter: Donald J. Trump and the Politics of Debasement," *Critical Studies in Media Communication* 34, no. 1 (2017): 61.

94. Stefan Stieglitz and Linh Dang-Xuan, "Emotions and Information Diffusion in Social Media—Sentiment of Microblogs and Sharing Behavior," *Journal of Management Information Systems* 29, no. 4 (2013): 217.

95. Kathy Gilsinan and Uri Friedman, "Donald Trump's Asymmetric War on the Establishment: The Logic of Policy by Tweet," *Atlantic,* Jan. 5, 2017, https://www.theatlantic.com/international/archive/2017/01/trump-asymmetric-war-establishment/512231/, para. 6.

96. Ibid., para. 6.

Chapter Five

Why Tweeting Makes for Bad Policy

President Trump's Twitter Campaign and Its Shortchanging of Critical Thinking

Dwight DeWerth-Pallmeyer

INTRODUCTION

On the day after he was elected president in 1968, Richard Nixon spoke to a group of his supporters about his hopes for his presidency: "I saw many signs in this campaign. Some of them were not friendly. Some were very friendly. But the one that touched me the most was—a teenager held up the sign 'bring us together.' And that will be the great objective of this administration, at the outset, to bring the American people together."[1]

Of course, when Nixon beat Hubert Humphrey in 1968, the country was deeply divided, particularly over U.S. involvement in Vietnam. Still, one sensed an honest aspiration for uniting the country.

Similarly, in his first public address after being elected, President Trump made this call as reported in the *Los Angeles Times*:

> "Now it's time for America to bind the wounds of division," he told cheering supporters at a Manhattan hotel. "To all Republicans and Democrats and independents across this nation, I say it is time for us to come together as one united people. It's time. I pledge to every citizen of our land that I will be president for all Americans."[2]

Despite that proclamation, one has never genuinely sensed the current president's desire for unifying the nation's divisions, especially while perusing his tweets. Many appear more divisive than unifying.

While both Nixon and Trump ran on similar law and order platforms, a more striking similarity in attempts to unify public sentiment used by Nixon in 1968 and by Trump in 2016 was to find a way to circumvent the established press, once regarded as the nation's fourth-estate. Both entered their election cycles with a suspicious, if not an adversarial view of the press. Nixon was leery of the press believing they were a big part of his failure to win the presidency in 1960. So he turned to direct talks with the American people or via one-on-one interviews on TV.

"'Nixon felt his only real shot was to avoid the press and go around it,' Ailes told Halberstam, 'and the black box was there.' Nixon's use of television in his first term as president was, with few exceptions, a success. But he just could not be happy circumventing the press: he needed to defeat it."[3] Trump has consistently accused the news media of propagating "FAKE NEWS."

COMPARISON OF TWEETS: CAMPAIGN TRAIL VS EARLY PRESIDENCY

For the presidential contender, Donald Trump, the favorite tool of media circumvention was the tweet. Much was written about the Twitter campaign in the popular press . . . the same press the candidate had regularly come to accuse as purveyors of "FAKE NEWS." Some thought the tactic was a mark of a political genius. For example, in late 2015, *Washington Post* reporter Amber Phillips wrote this account:

> One of the most central tools to Trump's penny-pinching campaign is Twitter. The 69-year-old uses the tool like a digital native, more prolifically than any other presidential candidate and arguably with much more skill.
>
> History will be the ultimate judge, but Trump appears to be on his way to becoming the first major U.S. politician to use it in a way that truly shapes—not just amplifies—his message.[4]

Phillips article went on to imply that one key function of the president's use of Twitter was to test ideas and to see how significantly they resonated with his audience. Another, she noted, is the validation it seemed to give him on a personal level, "It's almost as though Twitter and the validation he finds there fuels him."[5]

Indeed, the tweets seemed a fundamental forum for the Trump campaign, and his messages there seemed to draw a large number of followers even after his first 100 days in office. His personal Twitter site, @realDonaldTrump (as of late July 2017) reported a total following of about thirty-five million and his official site as president, President Trump@POTUS had a following of close to twenty million. However, with further research, those numbers appeared specious by many analysts. For example, a highly regarded analytics firm estimated that only four million (or about 10 percent) of Trump's Twitter followers were "active." [6] Another report from Bloomberg showed about 28 percent of his followers were "eggs" or fake profiles. The same report indicated that 80 percent of his top followers were fake.[7]

Of course, even during the height of his campaign's popularity, most Americans, perhaps even most of his actual Twitter followers, were not reading his every tweet, but the seeming outlandish nature of many of those tweets certainly garnered news media attention, which actually seemed to feed his new style of populism. What McCombs and Shaw noted decades earlier in their "agenda-setting" theory of the news media[8] proved to work in Trump's favor during both the Republican primaries and the 2016 general election.

In brief, the theory suggests that the media are not particularly effective in telling the public what to think, but they are extremely effective in setting the news agenda; they tell us what to think about. In 2015 and 2016, Trump's tweets became the news agenda and his somewhat angry, pro-American stance resonated with many disenfranchised voters who deemed Trump outside the status quo of Washington politics. But even Trump's own campaign staff was worried about fallout from some of his more controversial tweets.

They devised a strategy to keep exposing him to positive news coverage, daily showing him positive press coverage. The president-elect was more likely to fire off counterproductive tweets if he believed he was not getting favorable coverage by the news media. "If candidate Trump was upset about unfair coverage, it was productive to show him that he was getting fair coverage from outlets that were persuadable," said former communications director Sam Nunberg. "The same media that our base digests and prefers are going to be the base for his support. I would assume the president would like to see positive and preferential treatment from those outlets and that would help the operations overall."[9]

While the presidential contender may have effectively tapped into Twitter as his "go-to" campaign tool, it seemed a bit surprising that he would continue to use it so readily during his days as commander in chief because it clearly defies his stated intent for his time in the presidency. "In a 60 Minutes interview with Leslie Stahl in November 2016, the President-elect remarked, 'I'm going to do (tweeting) very restrained, if I use it at all, I'm going to do very restrained (tweeting).'" [10]

That has not proved particularly true. Indeed, in this chapter's forthcoming analysis of just his "personal tweets" (@realDonaldTrump), the president tweeted an average of five times in each of his first 100 days. But his use of Twitter did not seem to be a useful political tool once in office. The general consensus was that his use of Twitter during the first 100 days served as a political liability. Part of that may be due to tone. After his first fifty days in office, NBC News reported that the president's key antagonists in his tweets were: the media, celebrities, politicians, and on occasion, the entire American public.[11]

His popularity ratings sank precipitously, "A Washington Post/ABC poll released on Sunday [April 23rd—the 100th day was April 29th] showed the new president with the lowest approval rating at this point of any president since the polling began in 1945—42 percent of respondents told pollsters they approved of his performance thus far, while 53 percent disapproved."[12] While Trump never garnered high ratings, an NBC poll showed he slipped 4 percent from the end of February to the middle of April in American's view of his job performance.[13]

How much of that approval drop was the result of his communication via Twitter approach? Perhaps a sizeable portion. A poll in late June by Quinnipiac University made the sentiment clearer. Sixty percent of registered voters said they wished the president would stop tweeting from his personal account.[14]

It is difficult to assess the urgency or rationale the president feels in his use of Twitter, especially when it certainly has not seemed to earn him the political capital typically required by one who occupies the oval office. Yet studies have examined those who lean toward using Twitter as their primary social media venue. A type of communications research labeled "Uses and Gratifications"[15] theorizes that media consumers use the media consciously for different reasons or gratifications. In a recent study of social media consumers that employed a Uses and Gratifications framework,[16] the authors found that:

> Twitter users reported the highest *bridging social capital* . . . followed by Instagram, Facebook, and Snapchat. This may be attributed to Twitter being a micro-blogging platform, whereby users can follow other individuals with whom they do not have a real-life relationship, such as celebrities, politicians, brands, and organizations.[17]
>
> The diverse network of weak ties that Twitter users build on the site thereby leads to higher bridging social capital.[18]

Bridging social capital would indeed seem like a logical motive during a contentious election. It is typically defined as:

> ties between individuals which cross social divides or between social groups. From a network perspective bridging social capital places the actors at structural holes where each is able to tap into the social network resources of each other's social group. . . . Bridging social capital may not involve many shared norms but is likely to be associated with reciprocity and "thin trust." It may provide access to network resources outside of an individual's normal circles and as such can provide significant individual (and group) benefits.[19]

Despite its inherent limitations, President Trump leaned heavily on Twitter as a vehicle for conveying his ideas, despite his assertion to the contrary prior to taking office.

WHY CRITICAL THINKING MATTERS IN GOVERNANCE

While it is conceded that Donald Trump's use of Twitter was an effective tool in building a base of disenfranchised voters and both reinforcing and reifying voters' distrust of his Democratic rival, Hillary Clinton, it did little to clarify his approach to governing if elected. It has also done little to offer American voters insights into his overriding policies in both domestic and foreign policies and has offered little if any specific details. When a tweet is limited to 140 characters, as was the case during this study, sharing details is next to impossible if Twitter is the primary means of sharing information from the executive branch.

Limited access to governmental information seems to fly in the face of what Stephen Macedo labels "the dominant school of liberal [not politically liberal] political thought."[20] He writes, "Citizens deprived of the opportunity and the responsibility to grapple with the most significant moral questions lose a vital part of the training in responsibility and self-control that citizenship should bring."[21]

Similarly, Kevin Delaplane, who chaired the department of Philosophy and Religious studies at Iowa State University before leaving the formal academy, writes:

> As citizens we're not normally involved in drafting laws and policies, but we're responsible for assessing the laws and policies that our elected and appointed officials propose and vote on. And doing this well requires both an informed citizenry and a citizenry capable of critically assessing arguments, pro and con, that pertain to the laws and policies in question.[22]

The American founding fathers envisioned a democracy in which the people were active participants in the political landscape (though they were divided on how effectively the uneducated could participate.)[23]

The question addressed in this chapter is whether or not using Twitter as President Trump's primary means of sharing his ideas, plans, and understandings with the American people can allow for an informed electorate. One way to assess that is to determine if it is possible for a 140 character tweet to convey elements of critical thinking that would allow for an informed electorate.

Undoubtedly, the father of critical thinking is Benjamin Bloom, who wrote his taxonomy of educational objectives in 1956. In his *Taxonomy of Educational Objectives* he outlines six key components of thought: knowledge, comprehension, application, analysis, synthesis, and evaluation.[24]

While there have been revisions and criticisms of his educational taxonomy, his thinking is sound and still can be useful in defining whether the barrage of information to which we are increasingly exposed is logically sound. In Curtis Bonk's examination of various studies,[25] he notes the difficulties many have found in attempting to consistently and reliably identify whether critical thinking is being employed in a message and at what stage of sophistication. Many times a message can straddle two categories. Therefore, this study sought to use a simple content analysis method of coding President Trump's tweets on several measures, including critical thinking.

Three hypotheses were tested via a content analysis of President Trump's personal tweets during his first 100 days in office. Every even-numbered tweet of the five hundred tweets he published on his personal Twitter page, @realDonaldTrump was coded.

- H1: A majority of the tweets will not meet Bloom's standards of critical thinking.
- H2: Tweets that could fit the definition of critical thinking would be more likely to be categorized in the lower levels of critical thinking: knowledge and comprehension than would be in the higher levels of application, analysis, synthesis, and evaluation.
- H3: Given the news coverage of his consistent attacks, despite his initial call for unity, a greater percentage of the tweets would be divisive rather than unifying in nature.

HOW THE TWEETS WERE ANALYZED

The approach began with a simple description of Bloom's original taxonomy as depicted on a Wikipedia site,[26] tied to sound academic authorities. While Bloom separated educational goals into three areas: cognitive; affective; and psychomotor skills, this analysis focused just on the cognitive area, which is broken into the six cognitive skills of which Bloom originally labeled: knowledge, comprehension, application, analysis, synthesis, and evaluation.

The design was developed to determine what proportion of more than five hundred tweets from the first 100 days of President Trump' presidency simply met any type of critical thinking, and what level of critical thinking was being employed. (The full coding instructions and manual are located in this chapter's appendix.) As simple as it may seem, it took some tweaking of these categories to achieve a respectable degree of intercoder reliability. Overall coding of all five categories described below achieved an intercoder reliability score of 91 percent.

Using the admonitions of Clark,[27] the critical thinking category was coded with the understanding that Bloom's "categories can be thought of as degrees of difficulties. That is, the first ones must normally be mastered before the next one can take place."[28] The coding scheme looked at these five categories:

1. *Type of Critical thinking* (if any): While an attempt was made to restrict coding to Bloom's taxonomy: *knowledge, comprehension, application, analysis, synthesis and evaluation*, the majority did not meet Bloom's minimal standards of critical thinking. So additional informative categories labels were added: tweets that were essentially *self-aggrandizement*, *links to other posts*, praise for Trump supporters, and those that met none of those definitions.
2. Tweets coded as "links to other posts" were subcategorized as: *links to his other sites* (such as POTUS); links that were essentially *tied to his supporters* (e.g., "Fox and Friends"); *links to what he deemed as oppositional press coverage*; and finally to *links of no real substance.*
3. Each tweet was also coded as essentially an *attack* or *not an attack.*
4. Each tweet was also coded as essentially one that *served to unify* the American public, *divide* the American public, or *neither*. (Tweets that were considered an attack in category 3 were automatically considered as divisive here.)
5. Finally, a large proportion of the tweets during the first 100 days were decidedly critical of the press. If the term "FAKE NEWS" was used, it was coded as such; otherwise, it was coded as *not*, despite a clearly negative depiction of the mainline news media.

WHAT WE LEARNED ABOUT THE TWEETS FROM THE FIRST 100 DAYS OF GOVERNANCE

H1: A Majority of the Tweets Will Not Meet Bloom's Standards of Critical Thinking

Statistical Analysis

One sample Binomial Test: Critical thinking = 68. Non-Critical Thinking = 185. Two-tailed Significance level .000. *Reject the Null Hypothesis*.

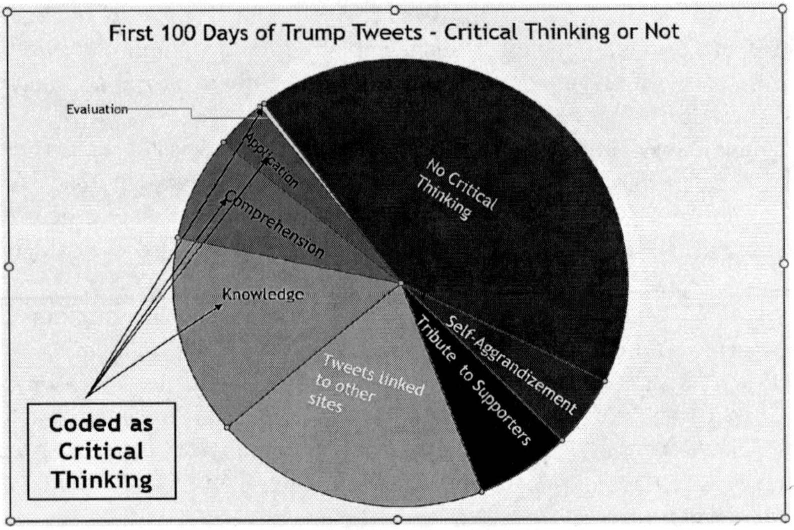

Figure 5.1. Graph of Tweet Analysis

The overall analysis demonstrates that a large number of Trump's tweets included very little of what could be considered as "critical thinking." Therefore, the first hypothesis was supported (as was to be expected). Critical thinking demands more than simple information, even at its lowest level. Knowledge, the lowest level of critical thinking, amounts to more than just stating a fact or opinion. Knowledge would have to entail at least some memorization of facts.[29]

Overall, the figure above indicates that the largest number of tweets were simply non-classifiable in terms of critical thinking. Thirteen of the tweets were labeled Self-Aggrandizement; President Trump lauding himself. Similarly, seventeen of the tweets praised his supporters. Forty-nine of the tweets were linked to another site, often his own postings on POTUS or to positive reviews he pointed to on *Fox News*.

H2: Tweets that Could Fit the Definition of Critical Thinking Would be More Likely to be in the Lower Levels of Critical Thinking: Knowledge and Comprehension than Would be in the Higher Levels of Application, Analysis, Synthesis, and Evaluation

Statistical Analysis

One sample Binomial Test: Lower Level Critical Thinking; Knowledge & Comprehension = 54.

High Order Critical Thinking: Application, Analysis Synthesis Evaluation = 10.
Two-tailed Significance level .000 *Reject the Null Hypothesis*.

Of the sixty-eight tweets that met some semblance of critical thinking, only ten were classified as more complex than simply "knowledge" or "comprehension." Nine of those showed some indication of Bloom's notion of "application." No examples of analysis or synthesis were noted.

H3: Given the News Coverage of His Consistent Attacks, Despite His Initial Call for Unity, a Greater Number of the Tweets Would Be Divisive Rather than Unifying in Nature

Statistical Analysis

One sample Binomial Test Divisive = 109 Uniting 88.
Significance .134. Do not reject the Null Hypothesis.

Among the 250 tweets examined, 109 were coded as "divisive," 89 were coded as "unifying" and 53 were coded as "neither divisive nor unifying." For the purposes of the statistical test, those tweets that were not considered as either divisive or unifying were deleted from the sample. While statistical significance is not established, one can reasonably speculate that a greater number were negative than positive in terms of a unifying theme.

MAKING SENSE OF THE NUMBERS

When the president of arguably the most important nation on the planet uses Twitter as his primary means of imparting important concepts, strategies, and an overall outlook for the American public, democracy is short-changed. Tweets limited to 140 characters are not an ideal communication vehicle for sharing complex ideas, problems, or for outlining strategies developed by the executive branch of government. Within a democracy, the stakes are too high.

While not winning the popular vote, the president indeed garnered the electoral votes necessary for victory. Therefore, he is the president of all Americans. Without adequate explanations couched in critical thinking skills, the American public has no legitimate means by which to assess the direction the country is taking and is therefore divorced from the very democracy Americans hold sacred. The same would be true of senators and representatives who use Twitter as their primary means of conveying their rationale for the votes they make. Furthermore, when the press is substantially locked out of the process and is often labeled conveyors of "FAKE NEWS," the essential checks and balances of the executive branch are put at greater risk and there is less room for clear accountability. (In this study, 17 of the 250 tweets included the phrase, "FAKE NEWS"—always in CAPS. In addition, there were numerous other critiques of the news media that simply did not use the phrase.

One of the problems with continually labeling institutions like the *New York Times* and the *Washington Post* as purveyors of "FAKE NEWS" is that many individuals also learn to doubt the veracity of the papers' reporting. That becomes particularly problematic when legitimately "fake news" can be disseminated by anyone who chooses to do so via the internet. Perhaps even the Russians?

"Reality" is never clear-cut. Each of our views of the world is socially constructed, by our peer groups, work environments, class distinctions, and so on. Yet, what most would deem outright falsehoods and false bravado, not only diminish the office of the presidency but also diminishes the way America is viewed around the world.

Just with a peripheral examination of four of his seven tweets from January 29 demonstrates the damage that can be done when pithy messages are delivered without further explanation, evidence, and forethought. And these tweets were by no means considered some of the most noted controversial tweets during the first 100 days. They were typical. In the first he continues his battle with the news source that likely garners the greatest American reputation worldwide:

1. Somebody with aptitude and conviction should buy the FAKE NEWS and failing @nytimes and either run it correctly or let it fold with dignity![30]

In the second, President Trump throws out a phrase that seems intentionally designed to alienate some of the nation's strongest allies.

2. Our country needs strong borders and extreme vetting, NOW. Look what is happening all over Europe and, indeed, the world—a horrible mess![31]

In the third, President Trump castigates legislators from his own party as well as Democrats and uses the scare tactic of equating senate investigations into starting a third world war:

3. Senators should focus their energies on ISIS, illegal immigration and border security instead of always looking to start World War III.[32]

And in the fourth, an example of self-aggrandizement is employed. Did the president really believe these teases would make for must-watch TV?

4. I will be interviewed by @TheBrodyFile on @CBNNews tonight at 11 pm. Enjoy![33]

One wonders if President Trump was employing some overall strategy behind this rhetoric or if it simply amounted to a stream of consciousness, voiced without concern for the comments' ramifications. In either case, the scenario is frightening.

Still, President Trump's style of conveying information to the American electorate cannot solely be blamed on him. There is evidence that today's citizen is often thinking less critically and therefore willing to tolerate a minimalistic news feed from the White House. One reason is that most simply do not read as much, and attention spans are shortening. A National Endowment for the Arts study released in 2016 found that U.S. adults who read any work of literature in the previous year plummeted from 57 percent in 1982 to just 43 percent in 2015. In some respects, we are all responsible when we fail to exercise critical thinking skills in our own lives and in our democratic participation.[34] This also marks a time period in which smartphones and social media are increasingly becoming the dominant way Americans are consuming the news. Additionally, there is little on Facebook or Twitter to distinguish reputable sources (typically referred to by President Trump as the ultimate purveyors of FAKE NEWS) and the less reputable.

David Edward Burke, president of citizenstakeaction.org, places blame for the election of President Trump on American voters' lack of critical thinking skills:

> In 2016 Donald Trump gave the worst presidential debate performances of any candidate I've seen in my 35 years. His answers were often incoherent and untethered from reality. He lied so much that he won Politifact's Lie of the Year award. . . .
>
> Donald Trump could not have succeeded in a country of critical thinkers, or at least in a country where enough critical thinkers routinely confronted those who weren't critical enough. Presidential debates and campaigns are only useful if the viewers are willing to analyze the candidates' answers, do their own research, and can tell the difference between facts and falsehoods. But we have not prioritized those skills in our schools and in our homes to the degree that's necessary for a representative democracy.[35]

That argument can also be circular. For better or worse, our leaders serve as role models. In fact, one might argue that an effective president should be displaying critical thinking in his messages to the American people, not only to keep them informed but to model critical thinking, particularly in hard times. How does the public learn to involve themselves in the political process or solve local problems cooperatively if the president models shallow thinking and appears to use his Twitter pulpit more often to divide than to unite?

There is a clear cost to President Trump's use of Twitter to wage battle against all those who disagree with his policies. When more tweets are divisive than unifying, it does little to build a unified sense of American pride and only serves to widen the gap between political rivals. Tensions build throughout the country and political parties attempt to craft legislation on their own. Compromise becomes a dirty word.

In a February 2017 article on the Brookings.edu site, Nicole Turner-Lee outlined the damage she saw with the president's use of Twitter inflicting on civil society. "Trump's use of technology, however, has baffled other domestic and global leaders, the media, and the public."[36] She goes on to demonstrate that his tweets have berated allies, endorsed companies, berated others, and targeted a judge who temporarily put a restraining order on his travel ban. She called Twitter, Trump's "megaphone to amplify personal grievances against those that dare to deviate from the administration's priorities."[37]

Such rhetoric might be expected from individuals at the Brookings Institute, an institution often seen as tied to more progressive ideas. However, it is clear that President Trump's tweets have also been a source of irritation, not only for those who work in his White House, but also from GOP legislators who see his tweeting as damaging the party and its agenda.

Perhaps one of the strongest pieces of criticism leveled thus far, in fact, comes from the noted Pulitzer Prize-winning, conservative columnist for the *Washington Post*, Charles Krauthammer.[38] In addition to his writing, Krauthammer is a psychiatrist who contributed to the DSM III (Diagnostic and Statistical Manual of Mental Disorders III),[39] the guide for assessing psychiatric disorders. He semi-seriously labels the president's consistent need to tweet, "Trump Derangement Syndrome."[40]

> It's the tweets, of course. Trump sees them as a direct, "unfiltered" conduit to the public. What he doesn't quite understand is that for him—indeed, for anyone—they are a direct conduit from the unfiltered id. They erase whatever membrane normally exists between one's internal disturbances and their external manifestations.
>
> For most people, who cares? For the president of the United States, there are consequences. When the president's id speaks, the world listens.[41]

WHEN THE PRESIDENT SPEAKS, PEOPLE LISTEN

Krauthammer is correct. When the president of the United States speaks, people do listen. Much is at stake. Miscalculations from texts sent early in the morning can send shockwaves across the world and certainly within the

United States. It is perhaps gratifying when one begins to witness members of his own party beginning to distance themselves from the president who seems to spend more time tweeting as some type of cathartic device for venting his frustrations than using his "bully-pulpit" in a manner that would seem to more effectively advance his goals for the country and unify rather than divide.

Many news outlets also have examined President Trump's tweets during his first 100 days in office. CNN, for example, examined the five hundred tweets and rather than categorizing them in terms of critical thinking, it determined that his tweets during the first 100 days boiled down to six categories: political comment or argument (165 tweets); typical presidential (142 tweets); self-plugs (86 tweets); complaining about the press (53 tweets); conspiracy theories (26 tweets); and personal attacks (18 tweets).[42] And while analyses like these are mildly amusing, they are also causing real concern.

The man who finds time for private tweeting to his followers an average of five times each day during his early presidency is the same man who reportedly only has time to read ten bullet points from staffers in the morning.

President Trump's tweets during his early presidency have been more harmful than helpful in conducting his duties and allowed him to deviate from his key agenda on many occasions. The same man who continually complains about "FAKE NEWS" is the one who has demonstrated his willingness to lie repeatedly. Frankly, the American people deserve more from their commander in chief. At the same time, a president is sworn into office is the appropriate time to stop tweeting and start engaging in genuine critical thinking and sharing those thoughts with the leader's social media faithful and the television networks that appear to operate as executive branch loyalists. The "leader of the free world" needs to actively employ critical thinking and share those insights with the American people. That is the least we can expect from our president.

APPENDIX

Coding Manual for the Content Analysis of President Trump's tweets from his first 100 days in office, based on how they do or do not display—Bloom's Notions of Critical Thinking.

(Much borrowed from the Wikipedia Entry on Bloom's Taxonomy)

Coding Category 1

Categories of critical thinking can be thought of as degrees of difficulties. That is, the first ones must normally be mastered before the next one can take place.

Bloom's Categories of Tweets

A. *Knowledge*

- Knowledge of specifics—terminology, specific facts
- Knowledge of ways and means of dealing with specifics—conventions, trends and sequences, classifications and categories, criteria, methodology
- Knowledge of the universals and abstractions in a field—principles and generalizations, theories and structures
- rote learning based on repetition

B. Comprehension

Demonstrates clear understanding of a situation, problem, role, etc.

Comprehension involves demonstrating understanding of facts and ideas by organizing, comparing, translating, interpreting, giving descriptions, and stating the main ideas

Example: Explain in one's own words the steps for performing a complex task.

(must provide some source of evidence)

C. Application

Demonstrates how a theoretical concept applies to everyday life, governing, etc.

Solving problems in new situations by applying acquired knowledge, facts, techniques and rules

Apply a learned abstraction to a new problem or solution to problem

D. Analysis

Breaks down issue, problem, solution in parts

- Analysis of elements
- Analysis of relationships
- Analysis of organization

E. Synthesis

Draws various components together to make an argument

In understanding a problem, solution, or situation

- Production of a unique communication
- Production of a plan, or proposed set of operations
- Derivation of a set of abstract relations

F. Evaluation

Makes an overall assessment of a situation as good, bad, complicated, simple, worthy, unworthy, etc. Evaluating involves presenting and defending opinions by making judgments about information, the validity of ideas, or quality of work based on a set of criteria. Its characteristics include:

- Judgments in terms of internal evidence
- Judgments in terms of external criteria

(some internal evidence or external criteria must be included in tweet)

G. Tweets lacking critical thinking
GS: Self Aggrandizement
GL: Mostly a link (if so is it linked to his own writings/tweets elsewhere?) (To praising a positive press?) (To something else.)
GP: Praise of his followers
GN: None of the above

Coding Category 2
Is the tweet an attack or not? Yes or No. (Anytime Trump levels criticism at an individual it is assumed that individual represents a constituency . . .)

Coding Category 3
Is the tweet generally more unifying of the country, dividing or neither. (If a tweet is labeled an attack in category 2, it will be by definition, defined as divisive rather than unifying). It is assumed that any individual who is attacked represents a constituency and is therefore divisive.

Coding Category 4
Does the president use the term "FAKE NEWS" in the tweet? Even if the tone of the tweet is negative toward the press, this is only coded as "Yes" if the capital words FAKE NEWS are used.

NOTES

The author wishes to acknowledge the dedication and his gratitude to his capable undergraduate research assistant, communication studies major at Widener University, Ms. Diamond Schuler.

1. Rich Kleinfeld and Stan Busby, "US History: Nixon Promises to 'Bring the American People Together' after '68 Win." Transcript in *The Making of a Nation*, Voice of America. May 9, 2007. Accessed August 12, 2017. https://learningenglish.voanews.com/a/a-23-2007-05-09-voa1-83134292/127719.html.
2. Seema Mehta. "Trump's First Address as President-elect Is a Call for Unity after a Divisive Campaign," *Los Angeles Times*. November 9, 2016. Accessed August 14,

2017. http://www.latimes.com/nation/politics/trailguide/la-na-election-day-2016-trump-calls-for-unity-as-he-wins-white-1478679682-htmlstory.html.

3. Thomas B. Beldon. "Presidential Press Conferences as Richard Nixon used Them." Ph.D. diss., University of Wisconsin, 1974.

4. Amber Phillips. "The Surprising Genius of Donald Trump's Twitter Account" *Washington Post*. December 10, 2015. Accessed August 12, 2017. https://www.washingtonpost.com/news/the-fix/wp/2015/12/10/reading-6000-of-his-tweets-has-convinced-us-donald-trump-is-a-social-media-master/?utm_term=.ef1374421cc94.

5. Ibid.

6. Jeff Nesbit. "Trump's Twitter Reach Is Actually Small," April 4, 2017. Accessed August 13, 2017. https://www.usnews.com/news/at-the-edge/articles/2017-04-04/donald-trumps-twitter-reach-isnt-as-big-as-he-thinks-it-is.

7. John Aravosis. "28% of Trump's Twitter Followers Are Eggs," *AMERICAblog News*. April 10, 2017. Accessed August 12, 2017. http://americablog.com/2017/04/28-trumps-twitter-followers-eggs.html.

8. Ibid.

9. Tara Palmeri. "How Trump's Campaign Staffers Tried to Keep Him Off Twitter," *Politico*. February 22, 2017. Accessed August 13, 2017. https://www.politico.com/story/2017/02/trump-twitter-staffer-235263.

10. Tara Palmeri, Jack Shafer, James Kitfield, Garrett M. Graff, Sarah Holder, Sheila Miyoshi Jager, and Rich Lowry, "How Trump's Campaign Staffers Tried to Keep Him Off Twitter." *Politico*. February 22, 2017. Accessed August 13, 2017. http://www.politico.com/story/2017/02/trump-twitter-staffer-235263.

11. Anna Brand, Sam Petulla, and Carrie Dann, "Commander-in-Tweet: 50 Days of @RealDonaldTrump." NBCNews.com. March 10, 2017. Accessed August 14, 2017. http://www.nbcnews.com/politics/donald-trump/commander-tweet-here-s-what-50-days-realdonaldtrump-looks-n731496.

12. Maxwell Tani. "2 Major New Polls Show Trump Will Conclude His First 100 Days as the Least Popular President in Modern History," *Business Insider*. April 23, 2017. Accessed August 13, 2017. http://www.businessinsider.com/trump-low-approval-rating-first-100-days-2017-4.

13. Ibid.

14. Melissa Chan. "Most American Voters Want Donald Trump to Ditch His Twitter Account:" Poll, *Fortune.com*. November 22, 2016. Accessed August 13, 2017. http://fortune.com/2016/11/22/donald-trump-twitter-poll/.

15. E. Katz, J. G. Blumler, and M. Gurevitch, "Utilization of Mass Communication by the Individual," in *The Uses of Mass Communications: Current Perspectives on Gratifications Research*, 19–31. London: Sage, 1974.

16. Joe Phua, Seunga Venus Jin, and Jihoon Jay Kim, "Uses and Gratifications of Social Networking Sites for Bridging and Bonding Social Capital," *Computers in Human Behavior* 72, no. C (2017): 115–122.

17. J. Phua, and S. V. Jin, "Following Celebrities' Tweets about Brands: The Impact of Twitter-based Electronic Word-of-Mouth on Consumers' Source Credibility Perception, Buying Intention, and Social Identification with Celebrities," *Journal of Advertising*, 43, no. 2 (2014): 181–195. Accessed August 13, 2017. doi: 10.1080/00913367.2013.827606.

18. Joe Phua, Seunga Venus Jin, and Jihoon Jay Kim, "Uses and Gratifications of Social Networking Sites for Bridging and Bonding Social Capital," *Computers in Human Behavior* 72, no. C (2017): 115–122.

19. Tristan Claridge. "Explanation of Types of Social Capital," Social Capital Research. May 26, 2017. Accessed August 13, 2017. http://www.socialcapitalresearch.com/explanation-types-social-capital/.

20. Stephen Macedo. "Introduction," to *Deliberative Politics: Essays on Democracy and Disagreement*, 3–14. New York: Oxford University Press, 1999.

21. Ibid.

22. Kevin deLaplante. "Critical Thinking for Healthy Democracies," Become an Argument Ninja. Accessed August 13, 2017. http://argumentninja.com/critical-thinking-for-healthy-democracies.

23. Alan Taylor. "The Virtue of an Educated Voter," *The American Scholar* 85, no. 4 (2016): 18–27. Accessed August 13, 2017. ProQuest Central.

24. Benjamin Samuel Bloom. *Taxonomy of Educational Objectives*. New York: Longmans, Green, 1956.

25. Curtis J. Bonk, "Super Summary: Evaluating Critical Thinking," Accessed August 13, 2017. http://www.indiana.edu/~bobweb/st_work/st_11/sm_st_11.html.

26. "Bloom's Taxonomy," Wikipedia. July 27, 2017. Accessed August 13, 2017. https://en.wikipedia.org/wiki/Bloom%27s_taxonomy.

27. Donald Clark. "Bloom's Taxonomy of Learning Domains:" The Cognitive Domain," January 12, 2015. Accessed August 13, 2017. http:/www.nwlink.com/~Donclark/hrd/bloom.html.

28. Ibid.

29. Heather Coffey. "Bloom's Taxonomy," 2008. Accessed August 14, 2017. http://www.learnnc.org/lp/pages/4719.

30. Donald J. Trump. "Somebody with Aptitude and Conviction Should Buy the FAKE NEWS and Failing @nytimes and Either Run It Correctly or Let It Fold with Dignity!" Twitter, January 29, 2017. Accessed December 14, 2017. https://twitter.com/realdonaldtrump/status/825690087857995776?lang=en.

31. Donald J. Trump. "Our Country Needs Strong Borders and Extreme Vetting, NOW. Look What Is Happening All over Europe and, Indeed, the World—a Horrible Mess!" Twitter, January 29, 2017. Accessed December 15, 2017. https://twitter.com/realdonaldtrump/status/825692045532618753.

32. Donald J. Trump. "Senators Should Focus Their Energies on ISIS, Illegal Immigration and Border Security Instead of Always Looking to Start World War III," Twitter, January 29, 2017. Accessed December 15, 2017. https://twitter.com/realDonaldTrump/status/825823217025691648.

33. The Trump Archive. "Tweet: January 29, 2017 at 03:39PM." Accessed December 15, 2017. http://www.trumparchive.org/2017/01/29/tweet-january-29-2017-at-0339pm/.

34. Christopher Ingraham. "The Long, Steady Decline of Literary Reading," *Washington Post*. September 07, 2016. Accessed August 14, 2017. https://www.washingtonpost.com/news/wonk/wp/2016/09/07/the-long-steady-decline-of-literary-reading/?utm_term=.6d3c7880d60c.

35. David Edward Burke. "Donald Trump Is the President We Deserve," *Huffington Post*. November 09, 2016. Accessed August 14, 2017. http://www

.huffingtonpost.com/entry/its-our-fault-donald-trump-is-the-president-we-deserve_us_58234923e4b044f827a795c6.

36. Nicol Turner-Lee. "How the President's Twitter Account Affects Civil Society," Brookings, February 16, 2017. Accessed August 15, 2017. https://www.brookings.edu/blog/techtank/2017/02/16/how-the-presidents-twitter-account-affects-civil-society/.

37. Ibid.

38. "Charles Krauthammer," Wikipedia, August 12, 2017. Accessed August 15, 2017. https://en.wikipedia.org/wiki/Charles_Krauthammer.

39. P. Pichot. "[DSM-III: The 3d Edition of the Diagnostic and Statistical Manual of Mental Disorders from the American Psychiatric Association]," Revue Neurologique, 1986. Accessed December 15, 2017. https://www.ncbi.nlm.nih.gov/pubmed/3787052.

40. Charles Krauthammer. "Opinion | You Can't Govern by Id," *Washington Post*, June 08, 2017. Accessed August 15, 2017. https://www.washingtonpost.com/opinions/you-cant-govern-by-id/2017/06/08/fad7a168-4c7a-11e7-9669-250d0b15f83b_story.html?utm_term=.ca7df45452cc/.

41. Ibid.

42. Gregory Krieg and Will Mullery. "Donald Trump's First 100 Days, in Tweets," CNN. April 28, 2017. Accessed August 15, 2017. http://www.cnn.com/2017/04/28/politics/donald-trump-100-days-tweets/index.html.

Part III

SOCIAL MEDIA

Chapter Six

Presidential Twitter Storms

When Is President Trump Creating a Storm?

Jennifer Grygiel and Regina Luttrell

PRESIDENTIAL ADDRESS

When presidents address the public, they often do so in an effort to calm or dissuade fears, empower citizens, and instill hopefulness and stability. For example, when President Franklin D. Roosevelt took office, the United States was deep into the Great Depression, arguably the most significant financial crisis in the history of the United States. When Roosevelt addressed the nation, he immediately attempted to soothe the fears crippling the American people by saying "I will address them with a candor and a decision which the present situation of our people impels. This is preeminently the time to speak the truth, the whole truth, frankly and boldly. Nor need we shrink from honestly facing conditions in our country today. This great Nation will endure as it has endured, will revive and will prosper."[1] Roosevelt delivered his first fireside chat by way of the radio in 1933 with the goal of restoring lost confidence in American banks and comforting the public.[2] Similarly, President Dwight D. Eisenhower initiated the first televised fireside chats to address the American people directly, while, President John. F. Kennedy's pledge to the public was a rallying cry for unity: "We observe today not a victory of party but a celebration of freedom—symbolizing an end as well as a beginning—signifying renewal as well as change."[3]

Recently, President Barack Obama's words echoed across the West Lawn of the U.S. Capitol on his inauguration day when he said, "On this day, we gather because we have chosen hope over fear, unity of purpose over conflict and discord. On this day, we come to proclaim an end to the petty grievances and false promises, the recriminations and worn-out dogmas that for far too long have strangled our politics. We remain a young nation. But in the words of Scripture, the time has come to set aside childish things. The time has come to reaffirm our enduring spirit; to choose our better history; to carry forward that precious gift, that noble idea passed on from generation to generation: the God-given promise that all are equal, all are free, and all deserve a chance to pursue their full measure of happiness."[4]

Each of the aforementioned rhetorical approaches may differ slightly; however, they all support a larger goal of rallying Americans to come together. Scholars have noted the importance of the presidential address to the American people. Matthew Eshbaugh-Soha observes "Speeches are vital to modern presidential governance,"[5] while Richard Neustadt, author of *Presidential Power: The Politics of Leadership*, was the first to contend that presidential power lies with public opinion and the way in which the president speaks to the people.[6] According to Theodore Otto Windt, with Neustadt's seminal argument, "presidential power is the power to persuade" he firmly solidified all presidents as the single most influential person who could motivate positively or trigger fear among the American people through their actions, but more importantly their words.[7]

The manner in which the president of the United States first addresses the public is important. Keith points out that "Three days after winning the presidency in 2008, President-elect Barack Obama held a press conference, taking questions from reporters. Three days after winning the presidency in 2016, President-elect Donald Trump turned to Twitter."[8] Amnon Cavari points out that "For decades, the power of the 'bully pulpit' was assumed to loom large over U.S. politics. More recently, a vigorous debate has broken out among political scientists as they attempt to redefine the impact of presidential rhetoric on the public and reassess its impact on public opinion."[9] Diana Mutz, author of *In your Face Politics* points out that "incivility" is often used in political rhetoric. She warns that it can be detrimental to facilitating respect for both varying political viewpoints as well as among citizens' levels of trust in politicians and the political process.[10] As researchers, we must examine the implications of a president that uses Twitter to communicate with the media and the American public, often in a hostile and aggressive manner.

President Trump indicated early on that he planned to use his personal Twitter account during his administration.[11] And he has. He frequently uses Twitter to communicate policy initiatives, openly defend his administration from what are perceived as attacks by the press, and even generate support from his base supporters. CNN pointed out that his Twitter audience more than doubled after the inauguration.[12] Given the reach of his tweets, and the perceived ability to not only "assign" the news but also provide real-time opinions that can impact everything from public company stocks to reputations, it is important to investigate the impact of a president who is a prolific tweeter.

This chapter focuses on a particular form of presidential social media communications—the "Twitter storm" and the manner in which President Donald Trump facilitates communication via Twitter.

DEFINING AND COMPREHENDING TWITTER STORM?

A Twitter storm, commonly referred to as a tweet storm, is defined by the Oxford Dictionary as "A period characterized by a sudden increase in the number of posts made on the social media application Twitter about a particular issue, event, etc., especially one that is controversial in nature."[13] This definition takes into account some of the key characteristics that we have come to expect in a Twitter storm, such as increased frequency of tweets around a controversy, but lacking any hard and fast rules and a more concrete definition, creates a situation where media outlets, the public, and the individual issuing the tweet debate whether or not the series of tweets can be considered a Twitter storm. Additionally, in the case of President Trump, he has stated personally that he does not "Twitter storm."[14] Many people may consider such proclamations as evidence that the president is not Twitter storming, and provides a rationale for developing a framework to understand when heads of state may or may not be Twitter storming.

An analysis on the frequency of postinauguration tweets sent between February 1 and July 17, 2017, from the preexisting U.S. presidential Twitter handle @POTUS (r=798) and the president's personal account, @realDonaldTrump (r=919), of which President Trump said that he was going to continue to use during his presidency,[15] was completed utilizing the social media data analytics program, Sysomos.[16] The sentiment and tone of the tweets were also analyzed to gain a better understanding whether the administration was using one handle to communicate differently from the other.

The @POTUS Twitter handle was selected as this was the same handle that President Barack Obama used while he was in office, and subsequently turned over to President Trump. Prior to Donald Trump using the @realDonaldTrump Twitter handle, a personal Twitter handle had not been used for presidential communication by a sitting president—this was a first. President Trump has clearly noted that there is a difference between how he uses social media compared to previous presidents. On July 1, 2017, President Trump tweeted out the following message that signaled that he considers his use of social media (e.g., Twitter) and presidential communications strategy to be "MODERN DAY PRESIDENTIAL."

> My use of social media is not Presidential—IT'S MODERN DAY PRESIDENTIAL. Make America Great Again![17]

In order to identify Twitter storms initiated by President Trump, the relative frequency of tweets was examined between the @POTUS and @realDonaldTrump handles to determine whether divergence exists when @realDonaldTrump had instances of increased tweet activity over @POTUS. Using the Sysomos "Compare Latest Activity" widget, specific days were targeted when tweets from the @realDonaldTrump handle spiked relevant to those from @POTUS. Tweets emerging from @POTUS are herein referred to as "traditional presidential social media," whereas communications from @realDonaldTrump are defined as "modern presidential social media."

Further classification of a presidential tweet storm is a day where an above average number of tweets from @realDonaldTrump is observed, wherein no less than seven additional tweets originate from @realDonaldTrump than from @POTUS. The number seven was selected as a benchmark given that the average daily number of tweets issued during this time period were 5.5 tweets for @realDonaldTrump and 4.8 for @POTUS. For example, a presidential Twitter storm would be considered as taking place if four tweets were issued from @POTUS and eleven tweets from @realDonaldTrump. Regarding the timeframe being analyzed, setting the benchmark of seven additional tweets initiating from @realDonaldTrump indicates a 46 percent increase over the @POTUS daily tweet average (4.8). Given the average daily tweets from both accounts, seven additional tweets provide a large enough spread that the two different Twitter accounts appear as a peak (also commonly referred to as a "spike") and valley in the social media analysis.

As a result, seventeen separate instances (days) were identified when tweets originating from @realDonaldTrump were substantially higher, relative to those issued from @POTUS; represented in the following image by circles (figure 6.1). An uptick in Twitter storms began in late May with the most intense Twitter storms taking place on June 26, July 1, and July 9, 2017. These days signify when President Trump issued ten or more tweets from @realDonaldTrump than from @POTUS.

It is important to note that numerous instances classified as presidential Twitter storms resulted from communications generally related to some of the president's more controversial beliefs and proposals, such as construction of a wall between Mexico and the United States and the so called "Muslim ban."[18] More recently, additional controversies have surfaced for the president, including the administration's relationship with Russia and pointed references to mainstream media outlets as continually reporting "fake news."

The following word cloud (figure 6.2) was created highlighting various keywords commonly appearing in tweets issued from February 1, 2017,

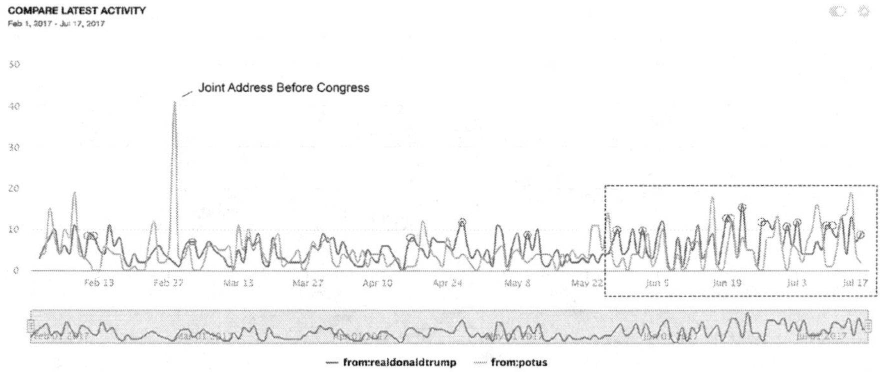

Figure 6.1.

through July 17, 2017, from @realDonaldTrump; many of which also emerge in the Twitter storms originating from @realDonaldTrump (generated using Sysomos).

For comparison, a word cloud was generated during the same time period for @POTUS. Some notable differences are the increased frequency at which President Trump mentions topics such as "fake news" and "security" from @realDonaldTrump, while the @POTUS handle tends to be focused on topics such as "weekly addresses," his "family," and "the American People" (figure 6.3).

The following tweets are considered Twitter storms initiated by President Trump. Included are examples containing tweets that appear frequently in the word cloud (from @realDonaldTrump) and focus on topics that are commonly debated by the media as being controversial ideas, practices, beliefs, behavior, or proposals, including "fake news," the border wall,

Figure 6.2.

Figure 6.3.

Russia, former FBI director James Comey, immigration, and other relevant topics:

Feb. 11–12: Tweet content re (referencing) the border wall, "fake news," and refugees

> I am reading that the great border WALL will cost more than the government originally thought, but I have not gotten involved in the . . .[19]

> While on FAKE NEWS @CNN, Bernie Sanders was cut off for using the term fake news to describe the network. They said technical difficulties![20]

> Just leaving Florida. Big crowds of enthusiastic supporters lining the road that the FAKE NEWS media refuses to mention. Very dishonest![21]

> 72% of refugees admitted into U.S. (2/3–2/11) during COURT BREAKDOWN are from 7 countries: SYRIA, IRAQ, SOMALIA, IRAN, SUDAN, LIBYA & YEMEN[22]

March 4: Tweet content re Russia

> Just out: The same Russian Ambassador that met Jeff Sessions visited the Obama White House 22 times, and 4 times last year alone.[23]

April 17: Tweet content re "fake news" and immigration

> The Fake Media (not Real Media) has gotten even worse since the election. Every story is badly slanted. We have to hold them to the truth![24]

> The super Liberal Democrat in the Georgia Congressioal race tomorrow wants to protect criminals, allow illegal immigration and raise taxes![25]

April 27: Tweet content re border wall

Democrats used to support border security—now they want illegals to pour through our borders.[26]

I promise to rebuild our military and secure our border. Democrats want to shut down the government. Politics![27]

May 10: Tweet content re Comey

Dems have been complaining for months & months about Dir. Comey. Now that he has been fired they PRETEND to be aggrieved. Phony hypocrites![28]

May 28: Tweet content re "fake news"

. . . it is very possible that those sources don't exist but are made up by fake news writers. #FakeNews is the enemy![29]

It is my opinion that many of the leaks coming out of the White House are fabricated lies made up by the #FakeNews media.[30]

June 2: Tweet content re presidential platform

#MakeAmericaGreatAgain[31]

June 18: Tweet content re Russia (i.e., "witch hunt")

The MAKE AMERICA GREAT AGAIN agenda is doing very well despite the distraction of the Witch Hunt. Many new jobs, high business enthusiasm.[32]

June 19: Tweet content re border security

. . . getting great border security and healthcare. #VoteRalphNorman tomorrow![33]

June 22: Tweet content re Russian collusion claims

Former Homeland Security Advisor Jeh Johnson is latest top intelligence official to state there was no grand scheme between Trump & Russia.[34]

By the way, if Russia was working so hard on the 2016 Election, it all took place during the Obama Admin. Why didn't they stop them?[35]

. . . whether there are "tapes" or recordings of my conversations with James Comey, but I did not make, and do not have, any such recordings.[36]

June 26: Tweet content re Russian collusion claims

> . . . under a magnifying glass, they have zero "tapes" of T people colluding. There is no collusion & no obstruction. I should be given apology![37]

July 1: Tweet content re "fake news"

> I am thinking about changing the name #FakeNews CNN to #FraudNews-CNN![38]

> The FAKE & FRAUDULENT NEWS MEDIA is working hard to convince Republicans and others I should not use social media—but remember, I won.[39]

> . . . the 2016 election with interviews, speeches and social media. I had to beat #FakeNews, and did. We will continue to WIN! [40]

July 3: Tweet content re "fake news"

> Dow hit a new intraday all-time high! I wonder whether or not the Fake News Media will so report?[41]

July 9: Tweet content re "fake news" and Russian collusion claims

> . . . have it. Fake News said 17 intel agencies when actually 4 (had to apologize). Why did Obama do NOTHING when he had info before election?[42]

> I strongly pressed President Putin twice about Russian meddling in our election. He vehemently denied it. I've already given my opinion.[43]

July 10: Tweet content re "fake news"

> If Chelsea Clinton were asked to hold the seat for her mother,as her mother gave our country away, the Fake News would say CHELSEA FOR PRES![44]

July 16: Tweet content re "fake news"

> With all of its phony unnamed sources & highly slanted & even fraudulent reporting, #Fake News is DISTORTING DEMOCRACY in our country![45]

> HillaryClinton can illegally get the questions to the Debate & delete 33,000 emails but my son Don is being scorned by the Fake News Media?[46]

Furthermore, in an effort to better understand tone related trends of President Trump's Twitter storms, an additional analysis was conducted (Sysomos) to examine the sentiment from tweets coming from both @POTUS

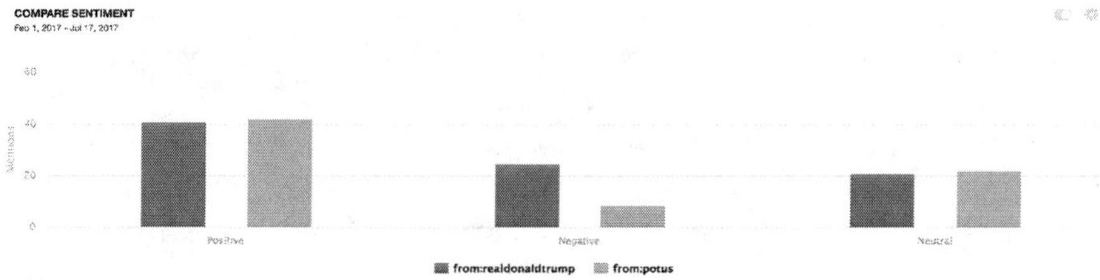

Figure 6.4.

and @realDonaldTrump. Figure 6.4 highlights that tweets initiating from @ POTUS (41 tweets) and @realDonaldTrump (42 tweets) were nearly the same for "positive" tone and comparable for tweets neutral in nature, but @ realDonaldTrump (25 tweets) had significantly higher occurrences of tweets "negative" in tone, than @POTUS (9 tweets).

The differing sentiments between the two Twitter accounts demonstrate a noticeable inclination for tweets classified as "negative" in tone to preferentially originate from @realDonaldTrump over @POTUS. The following example (figure 6.5) of a tweet coded as "negative" is included for reference (Sysomos). It was likely categorized in this manner as President Trump utilized terms such as "exposed," "garbage," and "fake news."

Figure 6.5.

Given that President Trump inherited the @POTUS handle from the previous administration, expectations of a specific tone may have been previously established among the followers of @POTUS. President Trump "split himself in two" when he started using both @POTUS and @realDonaldTrump for presidential communications.[47] The divergence in tone has been so notable that some have hypothesized that the @POTUS account is clearly being "run by his advisers, while the @realDonaldTrump account is run from the president's cellphone."[48]

WHY DEFINE TWITTER STORMS?

One question this chapter aims to address is, "Why is it important to understand when a presidential Twitter storm is actually a Twitter storm?" Given that this social driven phenomena is characterized as being controversial in nature and frequently reported on by the traditional media, it is necessary to establish some element of standards and guidelines when defining a Twitter storm. In the absence of a common agreement or measurement, efforts by the media to report on increased levels of presidential communication and public relations can and will be disputed (e.g., "fake news") and downplayed.

Strategy or Turmoil?

With the adoption of state-run social media (e.g., federal, state, and local social media accounts owned and run by the government), administrations are increasingly enabled to push out messaging related to topics of interest or even influence political posturing. Efforts to downplay, or in the case of President Trump, deny Twitter storms, indicates that institutions issuing a liberal number of tweets can promote a heightened level of PR and messaging under the guise of not actually doing so. This exercise can potentially lead to a suppression of news reports because media outlets are targeted as communicating false or incorrect assessments of presidential social media communication.

However, when looking at the data through an alternative lens, presidential Twitter storms may also be viewed as an indicator that an administration is experiencing turmoil; a potential rationale for why a president seeks to deny that a heightened level of Twitter communication should be considered a "Twitter storm." In essence, Twitter storming could be interpreted as being a defensive play, or on the contrary, simply utilized as a PR (public relations) strategy to further attract press attention.

In response to the increased focus on the topic, Twitter recently released a so-called "tweetstorm" feature that will allow users to release threaded tweets (i.e., tweets that are connected to each other) simultaneously.[49] The name of this feature is likely to create some confusion as the new functionality will serve as a way to "thread" tweets, and issue them at the same time. But it is important to note that tweet storming is also behavioral in nature and indicates a noticeable shift and uptick in tweets being issued from a specific account, not just the act of issuing several tweets at once. It is still unclear what impact this feature will have, but it is likely that this product change will encourage the release of grouped tweets, ultimately leading to a normalization of sending tweets in flurries. Even with the rollout of the new "tweetstorm" feature, it will also be important to understand when world leaders, such as President Trump, are increasing the amount of information they are disseminating. With that being said, leveraging an analysis similar to the one completed within this study, and following an appropriate framework for

Table 6.1. Twitter Storm Identification Framework for President Trump

Administration Twitter Storm	Tweet spikes from @POTUS on the same day. There may also be tweet spikes from @realDonaldTrump this day too
Presidential Twitter Storm	Tweet spikes from @realDonaldTrump *and* relatively low number of tweets from @POTUS in comparison on the same day

identifying a tweet storm (table 6.1), will aid in constructing benchmarks to identify changes in President Trump's public relations efforts and strategies.

CONCLUSION

The strategies in which President Trump utilizes his Twitter communications are certainly unique, and given his position as president of the United States, lends itself to a potential modernization of presidential communication, by virtue of the office. However, it is important to note that, in a historical sense, innovation and novelty have not necessarily always been associated with positive change, and with respect to this chapter, that Twitter storms are effective as forms of future communications. Modern communication is merely a state-of-play and represents the "present."[50] Theodore Windt concedes that presidential rhetoric "is only one of the powers available to the President, but in a democracy, it may well be the fundamental power upon which all others rest."[51] Therefore, we must reflect upon the magnitude of President Trump's Twitter storms and their far-reaching implications.

As noted previously, the following framework is presented as guidance in defining when President Trump is engaging in a Twitter storm:

NOTES

1. Franklin D. Roosevelt: "Inaugural Address," March 4, 1933. Online by Gerhard Peters and John T. Woolley, The American Presidency Project. http://www.presidency.ucsb.edu/ws/?pid=14473.
2. Tamara Keith. "Commander-In-Tweet: Trump's Social Media Use and Presidential Media Avoidance." NPR. November 18, 2016. https://www.npr.org/2016/11/18/502306687/commander-in-tweet-trumps-social-media-use-and-presidential-media-avoidance.
3. Tamara Keith. "Commander-In-Tweet: Trump's Social Media Use and Presidential Media Avoidance," NPR (Washington, DC), November 18, 2016.

4. "President Barack Obama's Inaugural Address," National Archives and Records Administration. January 21, 2009. https://obamawhitehouse.archives.gov/blog/2009/01/21/president-barack-obamas-inaugural-address.

5. Matthew Eshbaugh-Soha. "The Politics of Presidential Speeches," *Congress & the Presidency* 37, no. 1 (2010): 1–21. doi:10.1080/07343460903390679.

6. Theodore Otto Windt. "Presidential Rhetoric: Definition of a Field of Study," *Central States Speech Journal* 35, no. 1 (1984): 24–34. doi:10.1080/10510978409368157.

7. Ibid.

8. Tamera Keith. "Commander-In-Tweet: Trump's Social Media Use and Presidential Media Avoidance," NPR (Washington, DC), November 18, 2016.

9. Amnon Cavari. "The Party Politics of Presidential Rhetoric," *The Party Politics of Presidential Rhetoric*, 209–218. doi:10.1017/9781316576670.010.

10. Diana Carole Mutz. *In-Your-Face Politics: The Consequences of Uncivil Media*. (Princeton: Princeton University Press, 2016).

11. Jennifer Calfas. "Trump to Continue Using @realDonaldTrump Account as President," *The Hill*. January 15, 2017. http://thehill.com/blogs/blog-briefing-room/news/314440-trump-to-use-personal-twitter-not-potus-account-as-president.

12. Hunter Schwarz. "Becoming President More than Doubled Trump's Reach on Twitter," CNN. January 27, 2017. http://www.cnn.com/2017/01/27/politics/trumps-first-week-in-twitter/.

13. "Twitter storm | Definition of Twitter storm in English by Oxford Dictionaries," Oxford Dictionaries | English. https://en.oxforddictionaries.com/definition/twitter_storm.

14. Brittany Levine Beckman. "Trump Says He Doesn't 'Do Twitter Storms'—Uh Huh, Ok, Sure," *Mashable*. August 23, 2017. http://mashable.com/2017/08/23/donald-trump-twitter-storms-phoenix-rally.

15. Jennifer Calfas. "Trump to Continue Using @realDonaldTrump Account as President," *The Hill*. January 15, 2017. http://thehill.com/blogs/blog-briefing-room/news/314440-trump-to-use-personal-twitter-not-potus-account-as-president.

16. Sysomos is a third-party vendor that provides access to Twitter's firehose and analysis tools. This chapter, and analysis, utilizes this service and tools, and it is possible that at times the data may vary from Twitter's production environment based on Sysomos's API connection to Twitter and their sampling methods and tools.

17. Donald Trump. Twitter Post. July 1, 2017, 6:41 p.m. https://twitter.com/realDonaldTrump/status/881281755017355264.

18. "24 Things That Donald Trump Believes," 2017, *BBC News*. November 9, 2016. http://www.bbc.com/news/world-us-canada-34903577.

19. Donald Trump. Twitter Post. February 11, 2017, 8:18 a.m. https://twitter.com/realDonaldTrump/status/830405706255912960.

20. Donald Trump. Twitter Post. February 12, 2017, 7:14 a.m. https://twitter.com/realDonaldTrump/status/830751875578355713.

21. Donald Trump. Twitter Post. February 12, 2017, 5:19 p.m. https://twitter.com/realDonaldTrump/status/830904083519242241.

22. Donald Trump. Twitter Post. February 12, 2017, 6:55 a.m. https://twitter.com/realDonaldTrump/status/830747067379232769.

23. Donald Trump. Twitter Post. March 4, 2017, 6:42 a.m. https://twitter.com/realDonaldTrump/status/837991759045079040.

24. Donald Trump. Twitter Post. April 17, 2017, 8:17 a.m. https://twitter.com/realDonaldTrump/status/853945633903923200.

25. Donald Trump. Twitter Post. April 17, 2017, 9:31 a.m. https://twitter.com/realDonaldTrump/status/853964023846588420.

26. Donald Trump. Twitter Post. April 27, 2017, 10:39 a.m. https://twitter.com/realDonaldTrump/status/857605018266062848.

27. Donald Trump. Twitter Post. April 27, 2017, 10:37 a.m. https://twitter.com/realDonaldTrump/status/857604623531749376.

28. Donald Trump. Twitter Post. May 10, 2017, 3:23 p.m. https://twitter.com/realDonaldTrump/status/862387734492663808.

29. Donald Trump. Twitter Post. May 28, 2017, 8:45 a.m. https://twitter.com/realDonaldTrump/status/868810404335673344.

30. Donald Trump. Twitter Post. May 28, 2017, 8:33 a.m. https://twitter.com/realDonaldTrump/status/868807327130025984.

31. Donald Trump. Twitter Post. June 2, 2017, 2:30 p.m. https://twitter.com/realDonaldTrump/status/870709271477932032.

32. Donald Trump. Twitter Post. June 18, 2017, 6:38 a.m. https://twitter.com/realDonaldTrump/status/876388733607694336.

33. Donald Trump. Twitter Post. June 19, 2017, 4:27 p.m. https://twitter.com/realDonaldTrump/status/876899250071904256.

34. Donald Trump. Twitter Post. June 22, 2017, 9:18 a.m. https://twitter.com/realDonaldTrump/status/877878375045447680.

35. Donald Trump. Twitter Post. June 22, 2017, 9:22 a.m. https://twitter.com/realDonaldTrump/status/877879361130688512.

36. Donald Trump. Twitter Post. June 22, 2017, 12:55 p.m. https://twitter.com/realDonaldTrump/status/877932956458795008.

37. Donald Trump. Twitter Post. June 26, 2017, 9:05 a.m. https://twitter.com/realDonaldTrump/status/879324620159160322.

38. Donald Trump. Twitter Post. July 1, 2017, 6:08 p.m. https://twitter.com/realDonaldTrump/status/881273362454118400.

39. Donald Trump. Twitter Post. July 1, 2017, 6:02 p.m. https://twitter.com/realDonaldTrump/status/881271748280365056.

40. Donald Trump. Twitter Post. July 1, 2017, 6:02 p.m. https://twitter.com/realDonaldTrump/status/881271809433374721.

41. Donald Trump. Twitter Post. July 3, 2017, 5:10 p.m. https://twitter.com/realDonaldTrump/status/881983493533822976.

42. Donald Trump. Twitter Post. July 9, 2017, 8:06 a.m. https://twitter.com/realDonaldTrump/status/884020939264073728.

43. Donald Trump. Twitter Post. July 9, 2017, 7:31 a.m. https://twitter.com/realDonaldTrump/status/884012097805406208.

44. Donald Trump. Twitter Post. July 9, 2017, 8:06 a.m. https://twitter.com/realDonaldTrump/status/884378624660582405.

45. Donald Trump. Twitter Post. July 16, 2017, 4:15 a.m. https://twitter.com/realdonaldtrump/status/886544734788997125.

46. Donald Trump. Twitter Post. July 16, 2017, 6:35 a.m. https://twitter.com/realDonaldTrump/status/886534810575020032.

47. Suzanne Ciechalski. "How Trump's Tweets Have Changed in 100 Days as @POTUS," *NBC New York*, 2017. https://www.nbcnewyork.com/news/politics/Trumps-Tweets-100-Days-420623874.html.

48. Ibid.

49. Karissa Bell. "Twitter Just Took Another Step toward Becoming a Full On Blogging Platform," *Mashable*. December 12, 2017. http://mashable.com/2017/12/12/twitter-threads-tweetstorms-feature/#6u8m3Ykc9Pqc.

50. "Modern | Definition of Modern in English by Oxford Dictionaries," Oxford English Dictionary. https://en.oxforddictionaries.com/definition/modern.

51. Theodore Otto Windt. "Presidential Rhetoric: Definition of a Field of Study," *Central States Speech Journal* 35, no. 1 (1984): 24–34. doi:10.1080/10510978409368157.

Chapter Seven

Total Losers, Highly Overrated

Donald Trump and Internet Trolling in Real Life

Robert J. Baron

MODERN DIGITAL CULTURE

During the spring of 2016, I was teaching a class on digital culture and social media to a group of public relations and media production students. At the same time, Donald Trump was making his way through the crowded 2016 Republican Party primary season on his long ascent to the presidency. As one might suspect, these things frequently overlapped. The class had been created in an effort to introduce future PR practitioners, content creators, and social media managers to all of the "weirdness" of modern digital culture. Most of the theories, concepts, and ideas that the class studied and discussed during the term were attempts to make sense of, and, in turn, harness, that weirdness. As was inevitable, Donald Trump's social media campaign was a constant source of weirdness for the class to discuss. In late March of 2016, as Trump continued to collect delegates and the field of other Republican primary candidates continued to dwindle, the students were wrapping up a week-long class discussion of hacking and trolling; prompted by Coleman's history of phone phreaks, hackers, and internet trolls.[1] The class had spent the week talking about the cultural and technological aspects of hacking and trolling as they related to social media.

The students were familiar with hacking and trolling; several recounted recent "horror stories" they'd heard reported by the news media or seen shared on social media. That aside, some students were also able to recognize the value that modern digital culture often places on the "disruptive" power of hacking and the role that disruption plays in shaping and reinventing digital life. When the focus turned to Coleman's discussion of internet trolls, and the questions raised about the values and ethics of trolling, the discussion quickly became more controversial. Some students admitted to trolling, a few more seemed intrigued by Coleman's provocative suggestion that trolls acted as an online version of mythical and literary trickster figures,[2] but the vast majority had a harder time seeing trolling in any kind of positive light. While students were willing to accept the idea that *technological* disruption could create new value, they had a hard time seeing the kind of *social* disruption created by trolls as anything other than the work of a group of destructive jerks.

As the class continued to talk about what, if any, value should be placed on trolling, the discussion quickly turned to Donald Trump. One student asked about the things that Trump had recently said on TV and Twitter about Senator Ted Cruz. An anti-Trump super PAC had recently released an ad featuring a, seemingly scandalous, nude photo of Melania Trump from a 2000 photoshoot for *British GQ*. The ad suggested that viewers could "Meet Melania Trump. Your next First Lady" or that they could support Ted Cruz in the upcoming Utah primary.[3] Trump, in response, turned the full force of his ire against Senator Cruz, baselessly accusing the Cruz campaign of being the source of the ad, blasting Cruz in a CNN interview, and making the following, rather cryptic, threat on March 22 through his @realDonaldTrump Twitter profile:

> Lyin' Ted Cruz just used a picture of Melania from a G.Q. shoot in his ad. Be careful, Lyin' Ted, or I will spill the beans on your wife![4]

"What I thought about" all of this was a big question that didn't have an easy answer. While politicians have always dealt in their opponents' scandals and innuendos, these attacks seemed much more personal. Always one to redirect big questions, I asked, "Well, what do you all think?" The class didn't really seem to know how to respond, until one student observed that "He's just trolling" and that Trump was just doing these things to get a rise out of his political opponents. And there it was.

Everyone in the class seemed to understand what saying that someone was "just trolling" meant in the context of the internet, but it was harder to make sense of what that meant in the real world of American politics, where the consequences are far less ephemeral. As class ended, I observed that Trump was indeed trolling, but also added that to say Trump was "just trolling" seemed to brush off the real, fundamental questions of campaign decorum, our expectations of our elected leaders, what a politician's public persona should be, and just what the rules were for, what was becoming, an increasingly bizarre election season.

This was my first real encounter with the idea of Donald Trump as an internet troll acting in the real world. Like many Americans during the long 2016 presidential campaign, I had followed the Trump presidential campaign from its beginning descent down the gilded escalators of Trump Tower, through the string of missteps and scandals that would have, most likely, destroyed a traditional politician, and on to the Trump campaign's eventual electoral win in November. As the country moves deeper into the Trump administration's time in office, it is worth remembering that Trump's win came as a huge surprise.[5] Those that had placed their faith in the polling and statistical analyses that showed Hillary Clinton with a wide lead in several battleground states weren't sure what to think on the morning of November 9. Along the way, the question of what to make of Donald Trump's use of trolling tactics in his campaign stuck with me. What had originally seemed like a hindrance had become an asset. Clearly, Donald Trump wasn't "just trolling," he had trolled his way to the White House.

This chapter argues that Donald Trump has effectively leveraged the discursive style and tactics of internet trolling as part of his ongoing social media and political strategy. As the title suggests, Donald Trump was, and continues to act as, an internet troll in real life. To call Donald Trump an internet troll in real life is not to minimize, or excuse, the things that he has said and done during his campaign and presidency. Rather, this analysis seeks to understand what trolling means as a political discourse and what Donald Trump's use of trolling tactics might mean for America's political future. Put another way, this chapter takes Donald Trump's use of trolling seriously, and seeks to understand it, far from dismissing it as "just trolling."

After a brief discussion contextualizing trolling and its role in the Trump political organization, this chapter proceeds in three parts. First, it explores previous research on internet trolling and samples from some of the political and social commentaries that have examined Donald Trump through the lens of trolling. In doing so, this section seeks to better understand both the practice of trolling and Trump as a trolling practitioner. Second, this chapter develops a framework for understanding Donald Trump's use of trolling. It analyzes several tweets from the @realDonaldTrump account to see how Donald Trump uses trolling practices on Twitter for political gain. This analysis investigates the relationship between attack and engagement, through the act of trolling, as a part of Trump's campaign and administration communication strategies. Finally, this chapter examines what role trolling plays in developing Trump's social media popularity and maintaining the support of his political base. In its conclusion, this chapter also seeks to understand what Donald Trump's use of trolling, as one of the most amplified voices on Twitter, means for this social media platform, American political culture, and for the work of social media scholars and professionals.

This discussion of Donald Trump as an internet troll in real life has been started, stopped, scrapped, and restarted several times. In its original form, begun when the polls showed Donald Trump on his way to a defeat in the general election, this analysis was going to explore the ultimate limitations of using trolling as a political strategy. When Trump won the election, that analysis had to change. Later versions have coalesced around each seemingly campaign- or presidency-ending political crisis: the release of the *Access Hollywood* tape; the administration's clashes with the media over "fake news" and "alternate facts"; the ongoing investigation into possible Russian collusion; the firing of James Comey; the publishing of Donald Trump Jr.'s email chain; the collapse of multiple Republican attempts to repeal and replace the ACA (Affordable Care Act); Donald Trump's berating of his own attorney general, Jeff Sessions; the rapid-succession firings of Sean Spicer, Rince Preibus, and Anthony Scaramucci; personal clashes with Kim Jong Un; the manufactured controversy over NFL players taking a knee during the national anthem, and so on. Now, more than eleven months into the Trump presidency, it seems clear that Trump is a political survivor and, rather than a liability, trolling is one of President Trump's most potent political weapons. It is increasingly clear that the scholarly community needs to seriously consider how it views trolling as an integral part of Donald Trump's political persona. To ignore, or minimize, this facet is to miss one of the things that helped to bring Donald Trump to power.

THEORIZING TROLLING

While people have always found reasons to be purposefully belligerent, trolling, as a defined discursive practice, got its start in the early days of internet communities. Herring, Kirk, Scheckler, and Barab argued that they saw "Internet trolling as a manifestation of a much broader phenomenon whereby individuals take pleasure in disrupting the social order out of anger, perversity or contempt."[6] Whatever the root cause for someone to start trolling, Herring et al. went on to note that:

> It may be that the textual nature of computer-mediated disruption makes its strategies more apparent and leads to insights that would otherwise elude us in spoken interactions, but which can then be applied to offline as well as online situations. At the same time, the Internet poses unique opportunities for abusers and concomitant challenges for those wishing to avoid abuse. Among the challenges we see are the need to set clear boundaries on acceptable speech in order to ensure that civility, safety, and freedom can coexist.[7]

In many ways, trolling can be seen as a result of the relative anonymity the early internet provided its users. Freed from the confines of physical bodies and locations, internet users were free to explore new and different ways of interacting in online communities.[8] When people only knew each other through online screen names, it was easy to create and discard identities at will. This meant that it was equally easy to join and leave groups as one pleased, and act in ways that may have been seen as less appropriate in the real world.

Jullian Dibble's germinal article "A Rape in Cyberspace" is one of the earliest studies of "trolling" as an internet discourse. Although Dibble never invoked the word trolling, it is clear that the violent and transgressive acts carried out by LambdaMOO user "Mr. Bungle" against other members of the community were meant to be purposefully disruptive. As Dibble outlined, these digital rapes greatly impacted LambdaMOO's community of users and went on to affect drastic changes in the ways in which LamdaMOO was governed.[9] In another early study of trolling, Donath described the disruptive acts of early internet trolls as "a game" that trolls played within the confines of internet newsgroup communities.

> Trolling is a game about identity deception, albeit one that is played without the consent of most of the players. The troll attempts to pass as a legitimate participant, sharing the group's common interests and concerns; the newsgroup members, if they are cognizant of trolls and other identity deceptions, attempt to both distinguish real from trolling postings and, upon judging a poster to be a troll, make the offending poster leave the group. Their success at the former depends on how well they—and the troll—understand identity cues; their success at the latter depends on whether the troll's enjoyment is sufficiently diminished or outweighed by the costs imposed by the group.[10]

The best trolls are able to hide their trolling within the parameters of acceptable, normal interactions. Donath further observed that, because of this, trolling often eventually harms the character of affected online communities.

> A troll can disrupt the discussion on a newsgroup, disseminate bad advice, and damage the feeling of trust in the newsgroup community. Furthermore, in a group that has become sensitized to trolling—where the rate of deception is high—many honestly naive questions may be quickly rejected as trollings. This can be quite off-putting to the new user who upon venturing a first posting is immediately bombarded with angry accusations. Even if the accusation is unfounded, being branded a troll is quite damaging to one's online reputation.[11]

Golder and Donath reinforced this idea of discourse mastery and deception in a later work.

> For the Troll, then, communicative competence is the most important trait. He must be adept at understanding and using the styles of speech a community

> deems acceptable, so as to not appear as an outsider. The Troll is dangerous precisely because his identity as a Troll and therefore his true motive is not known until it is too late.[12]

Acts of trolling force online communities to make changes to the norms that govern their communities. In these cases, trolls were most successful when they best understood, and were thus able to most effectively disrupt, the discursive rules of the communities that they chose to troll.

In her history of phone phreaks, hackers, and trolls, E. Gabriella Coleman identified trolls as the latest in a long chain of technological disruptors. Just as phone phreaks and hackers used their understanding of dial tone technology and computer systems to "game" their respective technologies, trolls used their understanding of internet discourse and social norms to "game" internet interactions.[13] Coleman seemed torn in her classification of trolls as a part of this larger technological history. She raised the question: if trolls "deserve any place in the historical halls of hacking?" while, at the same time, noted that "underground hacking is notoriously irreverent and brash and thus helped to light an aesthetic torch that trolls not only have carried to the present but have also doused with gasoline."[14] As noted above, Coleman likened trolls to trickster figures. At the end of her essay, Coleman quoted from political theorist Stephen Duncombe in her observation that,

> If carried out responsibly, a politics of spectacle can prove to be an invaluable and robust political tactic: "spectacle must be staged in order to dramatize the unseen and expose associations elusive to the eye." The question that remains, or course, is whether there is *any* ethical substance to these spectacular antics, especially those of the troll, whose spectacle is often generated through merciless mocking, irreverent pranking, and at times, harassment.[15]

Coleman's later work examining the hacking and trolling collective Anonymous further developed this idea of the disruptive spectacle, looking at various attempts by Anonymous to upend the existing order online in the interest of their versions of social justice and internet freedom.[16] Whitney Phillips further developed this idea of trolls as trickster figures, noting that "trolls harness similar means to tricksters, resulting in similar ends. Specifically, trolls are agents of *cultural digestion*; they scavenge the landscape for scraps of usable content, make a meal of the most pungent bits, then hurl their waste on the unsuspecting populace—after which they disappear."[17] However, unlike Coleman, Phillips noted the relative normalcy of trolling, "while trolling behavior might fall on the extreme end of the cultural spectrum, the most exceptional thing about trolling is that *it's not very exceptional.* It's built from the same stuff as mainstream behaviors."[18]

Taking all of this into consideration, we can begin to develop an overall theory of trolling to guide our understanding of Donald Trump's trolling in real life. This analysis defines trolling as the deliberate disruption of a community's discourse toward the completion of some goal. In some cases, trolling is done simply for the troll's own amusement, or "the lulz." In other cases, trolling is done with specific goals in mind ranging from personal revenge to political and social activism. The trolls that do this best are the ones that have the deepest understanding of the communities that they troll. When changes are made to combat trolling, these changes can leave long lasting scars on the community's discourse. These changes to community norms, this social scarification, is the lasting legacy of trolling. While trolling may have started as a specialized internet discourse, the work of a few looking to disrupt specific online communities for their own personal reasons, it has now become more mainstream. One can easily log in to any social media platform and, without looking too hard, find numerous examples of trolling: everything from irreverent non-sequitur memes to flat-out insults. Like many digital activities, trolling has been democratized and opened by the development of social media technologies. All of this is important to remember as we consider the changes that Donald Trump's use of trolling has had, and will continue to have, on American political and civic culture.

TRUMP AS TROLL

This is certainly not the first commentary to look at Donald Trump's campaign and presidency through the lens of internet trolling. One of the constant refrains from the 2016 election cycle was to label Donald Trump as "troll" as a way to try to explain his behavior. For example, on June 20, 2015, only four days after Donald Trump announced his official entry in the Republican primaries, fivethrityeight.com founder Nate Silver declared that "Trump Is The World's Greatest Troll," highlighting Trump's ability to grab media attention and grouping Trump with previous "troll candidates" like Newt Gingrich and Sarah Palin.

> Trump has taken trolling to the next level by being willing to offend members of his own party. Ordinarily, this would be a counterproductive strategy. In a 16-candidate field, however, you can be in first place with 15 or 20 percent of the vote—even if the other 80 or 85 percent of voters hate your guts.
>
> In the long run—as our experience with past trolls shows—Trump's support will probably fade. Or at least, given his high unfavorable ratings, it will plateau, and other candidates will surpass him as the rest of the field consolidates.[19]

That Trump's support never faded, even as the political stage became less crowded, shows a deep misunderstanding of the role trolling played in the 2016 election and the Trump political apparatus. Similarly, Branstetter noted that,

> Trump has long been a real-life version of an Internet troll: Rude, uncaring, ubiquitous, and desperately confusing attention for affection. Much like many Gamergate aficionados, Trump is willing to be offensive and be derogatory if it means more people will see him, fostering a cycle that forces attention onto the ugly soul of a hopeless man. His presidential campaign is no different than a 4chan raid—an adolescent struggle for significance. To quote another rich man clinging to narcissism, "It is a tale told by an idiot, full of sound and fury, signifying nothing."
>
> But Trump resembles trolls in more than abstract ways, too. His media campaign for most of his public life has utilized the same methods to grab the attention and, at times, admiration of the American people as bored teenagers online.[20]

Both of these examples show a tendency to minimize the value and overall impact of trolling as a part of the Trump campaign. Put another way, both of these articles view Trump's trolling as "just trolling;" something that, while it might seem to be mean-spirited, hateful, and infuriating, is, ultimately, harmless and was largely politically irrelevant. In a follow-up to her previous cited work on internet troll culture, Phillips cautioned against such a dismissive and, in some ways, permissive view of trolling.

> Just as problematically, the "troll" framing—which is so often used with either the implied or explicit caveat "just trolling," i.e., "not a big deal/stop being so sensitive/learn how to Internet"—also casts aspersions over those who do not want to constantly deal with identity-based antagonism online. In short, referring to nasty online behaviors as "trolling" frames online antagonism as a game only the aggressor can win, most apparent in the phrase "don't feed the trolls."[21]

In another subsequent work, Phillips further argued that to view Trump as an internet troll, as so many analysts, commentators, and critics have done, was actually potentially dangerous. She noted that doing so limited one's ability to critique Trump and, too often, led one to dismiss his political antics as "just trolling."

> Furthermore, the notion that someone is *just trolling* establishes political, rhetorical, and affective distance between an individual and the things they do and say. The distance necessitated by the troll frame functions as an ethical escape hatch, looping one back to the rationale that if someone takes offense to an offensive statement, that's on them. When pressed, the so-called troll can always

point towards self-reflexive performativity ("I'm not a *real* racist, I just play one on the internet"), and away from personal responsibility for the impact their behaviors have, regardless of what their true motivations might have been.[22]

This is not to say that all scholars wrote off Trump's use of trolling as low-brow political theater or mere attention-seeking. For example, in an interview with WNYC's *On the Media*, George Lakoff took a serious look at Trump's use of Twitter. Lakoff presented a taxonomy that divided Trump's tweets into four separate categories: (1) preemptive framing of an issue, (2) diversion of attention away from a real issue, (3) deflection of an attack back onto the messenger, and (4) sending up a trial balloon to test the public's reaction.[23] In his interview, Lakoff analyzed the following tweet:

> Intelligence agencies should never have allowed this fake news to "leak" into the public. One last shot at me. Are we living in Nazi Germany?[24]

He argued that all four categories are present in this short 140-character missive.

> First, preemptive framing, this is fake news, secondly, diversion, it's gonna [*sic*] be discussed whether or not it's fake news or should have been leaked, rather than the content. [. . .] There's deflection, which is attacking the messengers, and then you get the trial balloon, will the intelligence agencies be stopped from doing this? Are they working like Nazi Germany?[25]

Oddly enough, some of the most insightful work examining the success of Trump's use of trolling in real life can be found in the unlikeliest of places. In an article on the humor website Cracked.com, entertainment writer Nathan Rabin offers the following evaluation of the effects of Trump's trolling:

> Trump was so endlessly entertaining, different, and, to use a word he angrily co-opted, *wrong* that the media could not stop obsessing over him. And throughout the campaign, respectable folks took comfort in the knowledge that Trump was too extreme, that his comments about Muslims and women and Mexicans and damn near everyone else rendered him unelectable. That turned out to be a false source of comfort. Extreme times call for extreme measures, and Trump really drove home the idea that we were living in end times, and that unless he was elected president, our country would burn to the ground and life as we know it would be over.[26]

That an entertainment writer, drawing on his experiences with the Juggalo fan culture, can offer deep insight into Trump's success as a troll, while many political analysts and commentators were quick to dismiss the practice, says much about the need for a better understanding of trolling as a newly-developed political force.

As noted in the introduction, this analysis seeks to improve our understanding of trolling as a political behavior and, thereby, limit the ability of others to label trolling in ways that minimize the impacts of these behaviors. If anything, labeling Trump as a troll increases the importance of the term. Examining Trump as a troll gives scholars a potent and meaningful way to label Trump's acts. Labeling Trump's acts as trolling also, reflexively, provides a means for a deeper understanding of acts of trolling online.

TRUMP: TROLLING TO ATTACK AND ATTACKING TO ENGAGE

There are two constants that run through Donald Trump's 2016 primary campaign, his 2016 presidential campaign, and the Trump administration's time in the White House. The first is his use of Twitter to critique, attack, distract, and otherwise "troll" his perceived rivals. Second is a sense of awestruck disbelief at the things Donald Trump has said and done on the political stage. Any attempt to understand Donald Trump as a politician must be mindful of how important trolling has been as a part of Donald Trump's overall social media strategy. In many ways, Trump's @realDonaldTrump Twitter profile serves as a direct extension of his public persona. Trump uses Twitter to amplify and extend "the Donald's" public persona from his raucous campaign rallies and his pugilistic interviews and debate performances. Trump blasts his opponents as being "crooked," "lyin'," or "light-weights"; calls out his rivals; and lashes out at those who he feels have done him wrong. In the worldview Trump presents to the public, he is constantly under siege: attacked by career politicians, corrupt government officials, and a dishonest mainstream media (or at least that's what he suggests on Twitter). This is not to suggest that everything that Trump does is trolling, or that trolling was the only thing that lead to Trump's victory in 2016; however, trolling remains a constant and essential part of Trump's political persona. Through the use of trolling, Trump both attacks his rivals and engages with his supporters.

Trolling to Attack

Perhaps the most outwardly obvious reason for Donald Trump's acts of trolling is as potent method of attack against his political rivals. From the early days of Trump trolling his opponents during the primary and general election campaigns, to his more recent attacks against his perceived rivals within the U.S.

government, in the media, and on the international stage, Donald Trump has consistently used trolling as a means for attacking his opponents. While there is nothing new with attacking one's political rivals, the style of Donald Trump's attacks are what set them apart as acts of trolling. When Donald Trump tweets at someone, it is often in the aggressive, disruptive, and personal style of an internet troll. These often-vicious ad hominem attacks draw media attention, serve to break down the carefully-crafted public personas of his opponents, and keep the public discussion from moving on to more substantive matters.

During the Republican primaries, the media attention given to Trump's trolling made it difficult, if not impossible, for more mainstream Republican candidates like Jeb Bush, Marco Rubio, or Ted Cruz to offer any substantive information about how their experiences in government had prepared them to effectively govern as president. At the same time, there was little Trump's rivals could do to demonstrate their conservative credentials, and thereby differentiate themselves from other candidates in the crowded primary field, when they had to constantly overcome dismissive and damaging labels such as of being "Low Energy Jeb Bush," "Little Marco Rubio," or "Lying Ted Cruz."

> Lying #Ted Cruz just (on election day) came out with a sneak and sleazy Robo-call. He holds up the Bible but in fact is a true lowlife pol![27]

> Little Marco Rubio, the lightweight no show Senator from Florida, is set to be the "puppet" of the special interest Koch brothers. WATCH![28]

> Low energy Jeb Bush just endorsed a man he truly hates, Lyin' Ted Cruz. Honestly, I can't blame Jeb in that I drove him into oblivion![29]

In the general election, it was difficult for Hillary Clinton to gain much, if any, traction with the general public when she was constantly needing to prove that she wasn't the "Crooked Hillary" character that Trump portrayed her to be on Twitter and in his campaign appearances. For example, Trump leveled this attack against Clinton following their clash in the first presidential debate over former Miss Universe winner Alica Machado:

> Did Crooked Hillary help disgusting (check out sex tape and past) Alicia M become a U.S. citizen so she could use her in the debate?[30]

Trump's response did not directly engage with the Clinton's critique from the debate that Trump was sexist, or that he was biased against Ms. Machado because she was Latina.[31] Rather, Trump personally attacked Clinton as "crooked" and Macado was "disgusting," sidestepping the critique and trying to shift the focus to his narrative of Clinton as a clueless and crooked politician.

Trump's use of trolling is not limited to only his political opponents. Trump often takes aim at those public institutions that he views as having done him wrong. Attacks against media outlets like CNN, the *Washington Post* (and its owner Jeff Bezos), and "the mainstream media," in general, serve to keep Donald Trump in the role of the dominant aggressor. In the following chain of tweets, Trump takes aim at two major national newspapers.

> The failing @nytimes has been wrong about me from the very beginning. Said I would lose the primaries, then the general election. FAKE NEWS![32]

> Thr coverage about me in the @nytimes and the @washingtonpost gas been so false and angry that the times actually apologized to its . . .[33]

> . . . dwindling subscribers and readers.They got me wrong right from the beginning and still have not changed course, and never will. DISHONEST[34]

In many ways, Donald Trump's political persona needs an enemy for him to attack. Thus, Trump's trolling is a string of provocations; Trump is constantly looking to be in a fight. While Trump's use of trolling keeps his political opponents on the defensive, it also serves an important role in framing the coverage of his campaign and presidency. When Trump attacks something through Twitter, whether that be a political rival, a public institution, a news outlet, or an entire political party, it makes news. In this example, Trump's attacks do not focus on any particular story, or take aim at any specific problem with these news sources' coverage of Trump, they are attacks against the news sources themselves. Donald Trump's use of trolling serves as an extension of the aggressive "fighter" persona that he presents to the public in his speeches, rallies, and TV interviews. These tweets serve to bolster Trump's own public persona, while, at the same time eroding the public's view of his trolling targets.

> The FAKE NEWS media (failing @nytimes, @NBCNews, @ABC, @CBS, @CNN) is not my enemy, it is the enemy of the American People![35]

This Twitter narrative of the constant assault, in terms of those both trying to "take down" Trump, and Trump punching back against his "attackers," serves to drive Trump's engagement with his supporters.

Trolling to Engage

One of the buzzwords of social media marketing and social media relations is the fuzzy concept of "engagement." The overall concept is that if a person can "engage" with their social media followers and connections, they will be able to better mobilize those connections to help spread a social media message.[36] As noted in the previous section, Donald Trump gained his political power by cultivating a public persona as a successful businessman and a tough, hard-nosed, negotiator. Donald Trump, the politician, is a "puncher," and he engages with the public as such. Donald Trump's use of trolling tactics, both on Twitter and in real life, are thus a way to enact this public persona, and to engage with his supporters through the enactment of that persona. Trump is a celebrity. His tweets are not the tweets of a politician, someone working to create a perfectly manicured image in order to remain in office; rather, they are the tweets of someone looking to engage with, and keep engaged, a group of fans.

This idea of Trump using trolling to engage with, and keep engaged, his fans helps to explain what has been one of the most baffling aspects of Trump's social media strategy: attacking the ghosts of his past political opponents. For example, in early March 2017, months after his inauguration, Trump took aim at the Obama administration by suggesting that President Obama had illegally "wiretapped" Trump's offices:

> Terrible! Just found out that Obama had my "wires tapped" in Trump Tower just before the victory. Nothing found. This is McCarthyism![37]

While this trolling attack, in part, worked to deflect attention away from the fact that the investigation into alleged Russian collusion was heating up, it also served as a way for Trump to revisit one of Trump's "greatest hits" from the 2016 campaign trail. Trolling to engage with his "fans" also helps to explain Trump's continued attacks and occasional legal threats against Hillary Clinton, long after her campaign for the presidency ended.

> Crooked Hillary Clinton now blames everybody but herself, refuses to say she was a terrible candidate. Hits Facebook & even Dems & DNC.[38]

For example, early on July 25, 2017, Trump posted the following tweet, reinvoking a campaign promise to prosecute Hillary Clinton for her "crimes":

> Attorney General Jeff Sessions has taken a VERY weak position on Hillary Clinton crimes (where are E-mails & DNC server) & Intel leakers![39]

This tweet does three things in one brief message. First, it brings up yet another of the constant refrains from Donald Trump's presidential campaign: his attacks against "Crooked Hillary" (and images of crowds of his supporters chanting "LOCK HER UP!, LOCK HER UP!"). Second, it attacks the perceived weakness of Jeff Sessions as Trump's "beleaguered" attorney general. Third, it also serves to distance Trump from any perceived failure to prosecute Clinton. All of these things work to engage, with and endear Trump to, his base of supporters. When Trump tweets these things, he presents his followers with ready-made messages that they can share and, thereby, help to spread his message. When Trump tweets, he tweets not like the typical politician, but rather like a celebrity trying to keep his fans happy. Like an aging rock star, Trump knows what his "fans" expect to see from him, and so he gives them what they want.

Social media engagement is a two-way street. Just as Trump uses trolling to engage with his base of supporters, one might also argue that, for some of Trump's supporters, offering strong and unwavering support for Trump is a way to troll the American political system. When viewed in this way, every time Trump breaks the norms of American political discourse, every time he lashes out and verbally attacks a political opponent or public institution, he only reinforces his support among this group. While Trump campaigned as a political outsider, several of his stances and expressed opinions are flat-out anti-political. Put another way, support for Trump is itself an act of trolling. When viewed in this light, what seems to be missteps only makes Trump stronger and more likeable in the eyes of his followers. Part of what brought Donald Trump to power was his assertion that he wasn't a politician, that he was the one person that could tell it like it is and drain the swamp in Washington DC. Donald Trump is not just an internet troll interacting in the real world in the ways of this online discourse; instead he is himself, a form of trolling. Donald Trump's election, and continued support by a die-hard group of followers, are a message to the American political establishment.

TRUMP, TROLLING, AND THE FUTURE OF AMERICAN POLITICAL LIFE

As I was finishing this chapter, the violent and tragic events of Charlottesville, Virginia, occurred. Once again, violent and vitriolic trolling spilled off of the computer screen and into the real world. It is telling that some (and only some) of Donald Trump's most fervent and vocal supporters come from the fringes of hate on the internet. This group has long lived in, and trolled others from, some of the less savory corners of the web.

While this work explores the implication of Donald Trump acting as an internet troll in real life, ultimately, Donald Trump is only a small piece of our larger understanding of what the discourse of trolling means for the American political sphere. In some ways, Donald Trump's rise to power is a smaller part of the story. The bigger story is that American political discourse has changed in ways that *allowed* Trump to troll his way into power. Trump was so adept at disrupting the standard political discourse and capturing the public's attention that no other narratives could break though in the 2016 presidential campaign. What this means for the future of American political discourse remains to be seen. What also remains to be seen, as the country settles in to the remainder of the Trump presidency, is what kind of president Donald Trump will be. Will Trump's continued use of trolling lead to trolling becoming a normal part of American political discourse? Is there a point where America will expect its leader to stop trolling and start working? Only time will tell.

NOTES

1. E. Gabriella Coleman, "Phreaks, Hackers, and Trolls: The Politics of Transgression and Spectacle." In *The Social Media Reader*, edited by Michael Mandiberg. (New York: NYU Press, 2012), 99–119.
2. Ibid., 115–116.
3. C. Eugene Emery Jr., "Donald Trump Has No Evidence That Ted Cruz Was Responsible for Naked Melania Ad." Politifact, last modified March 31, 2016, http://www.politifact.com/truth-o-meter/statements/2016/mar/31/donald-trump/donald-trump-has-no-evidence-ted-cruz-was-responsi/.
4. Donald Trump, Twitter Post, March 22, 2016, 8:53PM, http://twitter.com/realdonaldtrump/status/712457104515317764.
5. "2016 Election Forecast," fivethirtyeight.com, last modified November 8, 2016, http://projects.fivethirtyeight.com/2016-election-forecast/?ex_cid=rrpromo.
6. Susan Herring, Kirk Job-Sluder, Rebecca Scheckler, and Sasha Barab, 2002. "Searching for Safety Online: Managing Trolling in a Feminist Forum," *The Information Society* 18(5), 382.
7. Ibid.
8. For an in-depth discussion of identity and the early internet see Sherry Turkle's *Life on The Screen: Identity in the Age of the Internet* (New York: Simon and Schuster, 1995).
9. Julian Dibbell, "A Rape in Cyberspace," JulianDibbell.com, accessed August 10, 2017, http://www.juliandibbell.com/texts/bungle_vv.html.
10. Judith S. Donath, "Identity and Deception in the Virtual Community," MIT Media Lab, last modified November 12, 1996, http://smg.media.mit.edu/people/Judith/Identity/IdentityDeception.html.
11. Ibid.
12. Scott A. Golder and Judith Donath, "Social Roles in Electronic Communities" (paper, the Association of Internet Researchers (AoIR) conference Internet Research 5.0, Brighton, England, September 19–22, 2004), 18.
13. E. Gabriella Coleman, "Phreaks, Hackers, and Trolls: The Politics of Transgression and Spectacle." In *The Social Media Reader*, edited by Michael Mandiberg. (New York: NYU Press, 2012), 110–111.

14. Ibid., 114–115.

15. Ibid., 115.

16. Gabriella Coleman, *Hacker, Hoaxer, Whistleblower, Spy: The Many Faces of Anonymous* (New York: Verso, 2014).

17. Whitney Phillips, *This Is Why We Can't Have Nice Things: Mapping the Relationship Between Online Trolling and Mainstream Culture* (Cambridge, MA: The MIT Press, 2015), 10.

18. Ibid.

19. Nate Silver, "Donald Trump Is the World's Greatest Troll," fivethrityeight .com, last modified July 20, 2015, http://fivethirtyeight.com/features/donald-trump -is-the-worlds-greatest-troll/.

20. Gillian Branstetter, "Is Donald Trump the Best Internet Troll of All Time?," *The Daily Dot*, last modified March 4, 2016, http://www.dailydot.com/via/donald -trump-internet-trolls/.

21. Whitney Phillips, "Let's call 'trolling' what it really is," *The Kernel*, last modified May 10, 2015, http://kernelmag.dailydot.com/issue-sections/staff-editori als/12898/trolling-stem-tech-sexism/.

22. Whitney Phillips, "Donald Trump Is Not a Troll," *Slate*, last modified June 23, 2016, http://www.slate.com/articles/technology/future_tense/2016/06/the_prob lems_with_calling_donald_trump_a_troll.html.

23. WNYC, "A Taxonomy of Trumps Tweets," *On the Media*, last modified January 12, 2017, http://www.wnyc.org/story/taxonomy-trump-tweets/.

24. Donald Trump, Twitter Post, January 11, 2017, 6:48 a.m., http://twitter.com /realdonaldtrump/status/819164172781060096.

25. WNYC, "A Taxonomy of Trumps Tweets," *On the Media*, last modified January 12, 2017, http://www.wnyc.org/story/taxonomy-trump-tweets/.

26. Nathan Rabin, "6 Things Juggalo Culture Teaches us About Trump," Cracked. com, last modified January 14, 2017, http://www.cracked.com/blog/6-things-juggalo -culture-teaches-us-about-trump/.

27. Donald Trump, Twitter Post, February 20, 2016, 7:59 a.m., http://twitter.com /realdonaldtrump/status/701043432354095108.

28. Donald Trump, Twitter Post, February 28, 2016 7:59 a.m., http://twitter.com /realdonaldtrump/status/703974892237135873.

29. Donald Trump, Twitter Post, March 22, 2016, 10:07 a.m., http://twitter.com /realdonaldtrump/status/712728075532943361.

30. Donald Trump, Twitter Post, September 30, 2016, 4:30 a.m., http://twitter.com /realdonaldtrump/status/781784161044553728.

31. Aaron Blake, "The First Trump-Clinton Presidential Debate Transcript, Annotated," *Washington Post*, last modified September 26, 2016, http://www .washingtonpost.com/news/the-fix/wp/2016/09/26/the-first-trump-clinton-presiden tial-debate-transcript-annotated/?utm_term=.3f844aae866d.

32. Donald Trump, Twitter Post, January 28, 2017, 7:04AM, http://twitter.com /realDonaldTrump/status/825328817833123840.

33. Donald Trump, Twitter Post, January 28, 2017, 7:08AM, http://twitter.com /realDonaldTrump/status/825329757646618624.

34. Donald Trump, Twitter Post, January 28, 2017, 7:16 a.m., http://twitter.com/realDonaldTrump/status/825331665509691393.

35. Donald Trump, Twitter Post, February 17, 2017, 3:48 p.m., http://twitter.com/realdonaldtrump/status/832708293516632065.

36. This idea is explained in several books on social media. See, for example, Brian Solis's *Engage!: The Complete Guide for Brands and Businesses to Build, Cultivate, and Measure Success in the New Web*, (Rev. and Updated ed., Hoboken, NJ: Wiley, 2011).

37. Donald Trump, Twitter Post, March 4, 2017, 5:35 a.m., http://twitter.com/realdonaldtrump/status/837989835818287106.

38. Donald Trump, Twitter Post, May 31, 2017, 7:40 p.m., http://twitter.com/realdonaldtrump/status/870077441401905152.

39. Donald Trump, Twitter Post, July 25, 2017, 5:12 a.m., https://twitter.com/realdonaldtrump/status/889790429398528000.

Part IV

BUSINESS

Chapter Eight

Trump, Trucks, and Twitter

The Auto Industry Case and Presidential Speech on Social Media

Steve A. Stuglin

At 4:30 in the morning on January 3, 2017, President-elect Donald J. Trump keyed in his thoughts and posted them to the social media site Twitter. The post read: "General Motors is sending Mexican made model of Chevy Cruze to U.S. car dealers-tax free across border. Make in U.S.A. or pay big border tax!"[1] As of August 2017, the tweet has over 72,900 "likes," and has been retweeted over 18,800 times. The tweet was popular, but also represents a major shift in the norms of presidential address in the United States. That tweet is one of many in a haphazard, sometimes hostile, sometimes congratulatory series of Trump's posts directed at automakers. It is rare to hear a president attack or threaten an individual company in public and entirely new to watch it happen on a social media platform.

Trump's tweets about the auto industry are historic, whether or not they seem so at first glance. To support that claim, this chapter begins by establishing a crucial theoretical point: presidential speech matters. The next section explains why the auto industry is a vital subject for research to understand presidential address and how it relates to the economy. Although Twitter is the focus of this volume, Trump's more formal public speeches provide a useful comparison, so the chapter continues with an analysis of Trump's public speeches about auto industry issues during the first six months of his presidency before moving to Trump's use of Twitter. Ultimately, this analysis suggests that while Trump largely echoes former presidents on auto industry issues in formal public speeches, his tweets about those same issues are a significant departure from the norms of presidential speech, with potentially long-standing consequences for the norms of presidential address and our American political climate.

THE POWER OF PRESIDENTIAL SPEECH

The president speaks to the American people with special authority, as the president is our only nationally elected representative. The visibility and symbolic importance of the office lends power to presidential speech, making it a foundational discourse with the potential to guide other levels of discourse. Presidential influence might include signaling constituent groups, setting a national agenda, directly persuading and bargaining with other elites, going public to request support, acting through discourse as in the establishment of doctrines, the definition or redefinition of objects and events, or the construction of national identities.[2] Presidents can also frame events, are more able to frame events than are others, are more able to frame complex issues (such as economic policy) than others, and are more able to use exogenous events to political benefit.[3] By virtue of holding the office, an American president becomes one of the most significant voices in Western culture, and is one of the few people alive that reliably makes headlines worldwide.

There are limits to this power: within and across parties, with certain kinds of topics, against other influential voices, and with possibly limited ultimate ability to change the status quo.[4] Yet the potential for power remains, and there is evidence that in some cases, on some topics, and with some presidents said power is significant. Given this, whole disciplines have developed to analyze presidential speech in order to understand how it was constructed, what purposes it might have, how it attempts to achieve those purposes, and in what ways it had desired or other kinds of effects. This chapter contributes to that body of work by examining how President Trump continues in the rhetorical tradition of predecessors in one form of public address while drastically altering presidential norms with his usage of social media. Continued analysis of Trump's tweets and how future presidents choose to make use of social media will confirm whether Trump is an idiosyncratic aberration or whether his tendencies have become the new normal for the office of the presidency.

A FOCUS ON THE AUTO INDUSTRY

The American auto industry is a prime subject for analysis for presidential rhetoricians interested in the economy. The automakers that make up the industry in the United States are large companies—too large to ignore. They also represent a politically valuable combination of constituents, so politicians have predictably courted support from the industry.

Automakers are not as large as they once were, true. General Motors has been one of the largest corporations in the world, and was the largest automaker in the world for seventy-seven years straight, but no longer.[5] Automakers are not as large as some other employers, either. Walmart is the largest employer in the United States and employs more than two million people.[6] In 2017, American automakers employed just under a million people in manufacturing and another two million in various supply chains and dealerships.[7] Yet unlike Walmart, these companies make a variety of models of a durable good—something a consumer buys once every five to ten years and spends more on than anything other than healthcare or housing. When automakers do well, the consumers/employees they serve do well, and the country does well.[8] When automakers struggle, the employees and consumers struggle as well, and possibly the country.

The auto industry is also politically important. It is one of the few industries that has constituencies that have historically attracted politicians of every party. It has executives and blue-collar workers. Would-be elected officials courted the approval of those workers, with auto worker unions once being among the largest and most organized voting blocs. Would-be elected officials courted the executives, those leaders of the highly profitable companies that held power over regional economies. Today, the unions have shrunk, the workforce is smaller, and the companies are not as profitable, but political habits are hard to break, and politicians continue to court support from the industry. It remains one of the few industries with a long-standing political and rhetorical relationship to Congress and the presidency.

The auto industry is big and politically important, and when presidents talk to or about the auto industry, those two points are likely in mind. Given that, presidential address about the industry contains clues as to how a given president negotiates being tough with a powerful voting bloc, justifying policies that apply to companies with major influence on the national economy, and how the tactics for doing so are easily and often borrowed from predecessors that had to do the same. The next section includes an examination of Trump's public address about the industry in the context of similar address from former presidents.

SPEECHES: TRUMP IS MORE OF THE SAME

Trump is not an eloquent public speaker, although he is a frequent public speaker. His public speeches feature self-interruptions, tangents, and repetition of a small list of words and phrases. If one looks past these idiosyncrasies, though, Trump's speeches about auto industry related issues have not been all that different from those of former presidents. Presidents addressing auto industry related issues invariably choose from a small menu of topics: jobs, competition, regulation, and the symbolic importance of the industry.[9] When Trump has spoken in public about auto industry issues, he has largely followed the pattern of past presidents.

When presidents talk to or about the auto industry, they talk about jobs. The industry has historically been a significant contributor of available jobs, so this should come as no surprise. When Richard Nixon talked about the importance of the auto industry, for example, it was in large part due to claims that the industry at that point represented one in six American jobs.[10] Jimmy Carter provided jobs as the reason for intervening to help Chrysler in 1979, and this claim was repeated by George W. Bush and Barack Obama when each decided to help the industry in 2008 and 2009.[11] Jobs are a high priority issue for Trump, and he certainly talks about jobs when talking about the auto industry. Trump promised to bring auto industry jobs back or claimed they were already coming back because of him in at least eight separate speeches in February 2017.[12]

When jobs are lost in the auto industry, Republican presidents have tended to blame regulations. Nixon, when asked about regulations on the auto industry, said "when the Congress . . . sets certain standards to clean up the air or clean up the water, we must weigh against that: how many jobs is it going to cost?"[13] Ronald Reagan also targeted safety and environmental regulations when he acted to help the auto industry in 1981.[14] Trump's first six months in office have echoed that argument: auto jobs are lost to overbearing regulations. Speaking in Ypsilanti, not far from Detroit, Michigan, Trump promised to "eliminate the industry-killing regulations," to "identify and remove any regulation that undermines American auto production," and to delay implementation of others, such as fuel efficiency requirements.[15] Trump repeated these promises in other speeches.[16] Barack Obama chose to blame the industry itself rather than regulations, so Trump sounds typical of Republicans here, but not all presidents.[17]

Presidents have historically blamed foreign competition for the loss of auto industry jobs as well. Carter pointed to pressure from Japanese imports in his attempts to aid automakers.[18] Reagan famously instituted "voluntary" import quotas against Japanese imports, although he chose not to discuss them at length publicly to protect his status as a free-trade enthusiast.[19] Trump has frequently echoed this argument: Mexico and China took all of the auto industry jobs.[20] Although Trump broadly claims that Mexico and China are at fault for many of the problems in the United States, he singles those countries out for blame on the loss of American manufacturing jobs and specifically auto industry jobs.

When presidents talk to the industry or about the industry, they often stress the symbolic importance of automakers, autoworkers, and autos in general.

Since William Howard Taft ushered in the "motoring presidency" with praise of automobiles and the jobs the industry would bring,[21] presidents have publicly praised the auto industry. Franklin D. Roosevelt called for the conversion of factories of every kind to war production during World War II under the label "Arsenal of Democracy." Presidents since John F. Kennedy have instead used that famous term to specifically refer to the remarkable war production from the auto industry, using it as justification for all sorts of aid to the industry when it was needed.[22] Trump has copied this pattern as well, thanking auto workers and the famous Rosie the Riveter (a worker at the Ford Motor Company owned Willow Run bomber plant in Michigan) for service as the arsenal of democracy.[23] For Trump, as with so many things he describes with similar vocabulary: "There is no more beautiful sight than an American-made car. No more beautiful sight."[24] As early as December 2008, while the Bush administration provided aid to the crumbling auto industry and Obama, then president-elect, developed plans for aiding the automakers in 2009, Trump told *Fox News* "I think the government should stand behind them 100 percent. You cannot lose the auto companies. They're great. They make wonderful products."[25] Trump claims to love cars, automakers, and the industry—not unlike the claims of many of his predecessors.

Trump has sounded remarkably similar to other presidents during the first six months of his presidency, on auto industry issues at least. He addressed the same standard topics that other presidents typically address: jobs, regulation, competition, and the symbolic importance of the industry. He talks about those issues in fairly typical ways. In public speeches, there is little of note from Trump on the auto industry that Americans have not heard from other presidents. The next sections demonstrate that the opposite is true of Trump on Twitter.

PRESIDENTS AND SOCIAL MEDIA

All American presidents gave public speeches, especially since the development of radio and television helped usher in the rhetorical presidency, wherein presidential power increasingly became the power of presidents to speak directly to the masses. Rhetoricians have tens of thousands of speeches to analyze when searching for explanations and the buried mechanics of persuasion. Social media has only been around for a few presidents, though. Facebook opened to the public in 2006, the same year that Twitter was launched. Given this small sample size, we must be cautious with any claims about how presidents use social media to engage the public. To date, only four presidents have truly engaged the public on social media: Clinton, Bush,

Obama, and now Trump. Preliminary conclusions based on this small sample size suggest that social media is accessible, political, authentic (or providing the illusion of authenticity), and has the same potential power to persuade as other forms of public address. Each of these findings is worth a closer look.

First, social media accounts provide accessibility. Once you follow or friend a politician on a social media site, you are connected to them and to the information they provide. You can access this information across time and space. According to Gina Masullo Chen, this accessibility provides users a much needed form of immediate connection, which is what keeps bringing people back to the service.[26] The ability of users to then share the information provides a sense of engagement, bringing users into the political process without leaving the couch.[27] The exchange creates a bond between the follower and the followed, bringing a president into American living rooms, not unlike that created by Franklin D. Roosevelt's fireside chats.

This accessible form of connection is increasingly used for politics. Journalists flock to Twitter to discuss news, and in 2015 were the largest group on the site.[28] Twitter may be growing in 2017 *because* of politics.[29] Social media platforms like Twitter have become a core part of the political process—with politicians maintaining active accounts, journalists using the platforms to disseminate information, and the public using the platforms to connect to the process. Researchers have been able to match tweet volume with vote preference and poll numbers—finding that the former is a good metric for the latter.[30] Still, Kyle Leighton and David Taintor, among others, argue that there is a disconnect between political tweets, political energy, and voter turnout, demonstrating that more work needs to be done before we put too much stock in social media and its ability to shape elections.[31]

If Americans are using social media platforms as an accessible way to connect to politicians, then Americans will be looking for authenticity in those social media posts. American politics involves a predisposition for authenticity.[32] We want authentic or "real" politicians, and yet our media culture is always recording, making the letting down of one's guard a grave risk. This has led to "authenticity" presented under tightly controlled conditions. In 2007, at the end of the Bush administration, Gary Woodward wrote that there are "unchanging tensions created by the ritual cynicism of most of the press and the White House's attempts to counter it by organizing events that avoid the risks of unscripted encounters."[33] As presidential appearances are ever more tightly controlled in the post-9/11 security climate, and as those appearances are increasingly scripted and stage-directed, Americans are left longing for "real" moments that are very difficult to find.

Social media promises to serve the American predisposition for authenticity in its presidents, yet much of what we have seen is merely an illusion of authenticity. Those presidents that have chosen to use social media have largely used it to repeat shortened versions of already vetted statements—a snippet of a speech or a congratulatory cheer retweeting something from a powerful part of the base—things that are far from authentic or intimate. George W. Bush has appeared to use social media in his post-presidency, as has Bill Clinton, and those personal accounts often contain seemingly authentic moments.[34] Trump has, to date, embraced the authenticity Twitter allows, and given the controversy over some tweets, the public has little doubt that Trump is frequently, if not always, typing out tweets himself.[35]

Whether the politician uses social media themselves or has staffers manage the account, the produced messages can function similarly to traditional public address. Janet Johnson argued that Mitt Romney's tweets, while campaigning for the presidency in 2012, showed clear attempts to build credibility, express reasoning, and connect with the audience emotionally, otherwise known as the core Aristotelian means of persuasion.[36] Tweets from politicians can be just as divisive and hyper partisan as public address, according to Annelise Russell.[37] In the case of Trump, early research indicates that tweets are even more divisive and negative than standard public address.[38] Brian Ott argued that the format on Twitter actually encourages "simple, impulsive, and uncivil" discourse, which Ott sees as a natural fit for Trump.[39] This format, according to Neil Savage, also makes ambiguity and misunderstanding a frequent by-product of Twitter.[40] So tweets, like other forms of public address, can persuade, unite, and divide, and by their nature are likely to be simpler, less thought-through, and more easily misunderstood.

On Twitter, Trump is accessible, political, authentic in a fashion, and actively attempting to persuade. Trump *is* Twitter. While he has largely echoed the sentiments of predecessors on auto industry issues in more formal public address, his usage of Twitter demonstrates a very different approach. On auto industry issues at least, Trump's tweets are nothing like we have seen with any president.

TWEETS: TRUMP IS A SIGNIFICANT DEPARTURE FROM THE NORM

Trump is now the second president to make heavy use of Twitter, and his tweets about auto industry issues are a large enough sample that they can be analyzed for trends and mechanics. This section includes an analysis of Trump's Twitter presence compared to that of former presidents. The analysis shows that Trump's tweets are individually targeted, threatening and negative, possibly a negotiating tactic, eager to claim credit and avoid responsibility, less likely to include useful details than would be expected, and ambiguous. Trump's tweets are a troubling development for these reasons, given that they will likely lead to altered rhetorical norms in the presidency and further hyper partisanship.

Trump tweets more than other former presidents, but not as much more as one might think. Bill Clinton joined Twitter in 2013, Barack Obama in 2007, and Donald Trump in 2009. Clinton had 600 tweets as of August 2017, while Obama had 15,500 and Trump had 35,500. Clinton had a much smaller audience (8 million followers) than Trump (35 million) but Obama had by far the largest (95 million), the third most in the world behind Katy Perry and Justin Bieber, and ten million more than fourth place Taylor Swift.[41] Obama also had access to the @POTUS Twitter account for eight years, adding 500 tweets for a total of 20,000. Trump has tweeted slightly more often than Bieber, who has 30,000 tweets since joining the same year as Trump. So, while Trump has tweeted more than Obama (to a smaller audience, too), he is in the range of what we might expect out of presidents in the social media age.

What is abnormal is that Trump uses tweets more than typical public speaking to talk about the auto industry and when he does so he tweets with mentions of specific brands and companies, rather than reference to the industry as a whole. For comparison, while running for reelection in 2012, Obama delivered 885 speeches and 195 of them included the auto industry. In other words, in a little more than one out of every five speeches for nearly a year, Obama mentioned the auto industry.[42] In practically every one of those speeches he featured the positive turnaround at General Motors and Chrysler. During the same time period, he only tweeted thirty-two times about the auto industry, and only fourteen times making mention of a specific automaker (mostly GM). Obama used Twitter sixteen times less frequently than speeches to say something about the auto industry. If one wanted to understand Obama's rhetoric about the industry, then speeches would be the place to go. In the last year, Trump has given twenty speeches mentioning the auto industry but has tweeted twenty-one times about the auto industry, and in twenty of those twenty-one tweets made specific mention of an automaker (mostly Ford). Trump has used Twitter and speeches evenly to talk about the auto industry, so both are vital texts for understand Trump's rhetoric about the industry.

Given his reliance on Twitter, it is worrying that one of the chief features of Trump's tweets about the auto industry have been threats. On January 5, 2017, Trump tweeted: "Toyota Motor said will build a new plant in Baja, Mexico, to build Corolla cars for U.S. NO Way! Build plant in U.S. or pay big border tax."[43] Trump directed the same threat to General Motors on January 3, 2017.[44] This style of threatening retaliation directed at individual companies has been going on for years. For example, early in his presidential campaign,

Trump threatened Ford over moving jobs to Mexico, claiming it would stop on his first day in office once he was elected.[45] Tweets like this are so unusual of national politicians that they led Ben White and Lorraine Woellert of *Politico* to claim that "Trump is quickly putting the bully in the bully pulpit."[46] Of course it is not news when a president demonstrates strength in public address. Presidential power is, after all, largely attained and exercised through speech. Announcing policy in a threat directed at an individual company is decidedly less common, though.

It may be that Trump never meant for the tweet-threats to be taken seriously. Back in 1992, Trump and Tony Schwartz wrote *The Art of the Deal*, which purportedly claimed all of Trump's secrets for business deals. Two of the lessons of that book are indicative of what may have inspired these tweet-threats. First, Trump advised readers to "use your leverage."[47] Convince the other party you are coming from a position of strength and have something they need, according to this rule. If you have to blur reality to make the case, as Trump explained in an example about a Holiday Inn deal, so be it. In the case of the tweets threatening the automakers, leverage is part of the 140 characters Trump chose to include. When Trump became president, there would be consequences for certain actions, the tweets said. There is a second lesson from *The Art of the Deal* that may be instructive, too: maximize your options. "I keep a lot of balls in the air," Trump wrote, "because most deals fall out, no matter how promising they seem at first. In addition, once I've made a deal, I always come up with at least a half dozen approaches to making it work, because anything can happen, even to the best-laid plans."[48] The border tax threat was a useful way of trying to "make a deal" with the companies that were moving jobs out of the country. If it did not work as intended, Trump would not feel bound to enact such a tax, as there are always other options. In fact, Trump has dropped the issue of an import border tax, even though no major changes in auto industry employment have happened since the threats on Twitter.[49]

Some minor changes in employment *have* happened, and they demonstrate the next major aberration of presidential address on social media from Trump: the breakneck race to publicly take credit developments. For example, in late 2015, Trump took credit for his "constant badgering at packed events," which caused Ford to "cancel their deal to go to Mexico."[50] Three minutes later, he claimed on Twitter that he did not care whether he got credit.[51] In late 2016, Trump tweeted that Bill Ford, chairman of Ford, "advised me that he will be keeping the Lincoln plant in Kentucky—no Mexico."[52] Trump said he was "advised" of the decision, but he still took credit for it on Twitter fourteen minutes later: "I worked hard with Bill Ford to keep Lincoln plant in Kentucky. I owed it to the great State of Kentucky for their confidence in me!"[53]

Although Trump's threats of a border tax and his "constant badgering" on the campaign trail *may have* had an effect on the attitude of those in leadership at Ford, Trump likely had no direct influence on a decision to keep Ford from moving a plant from Kentucky to Mexico, because that was not possible. Under United Auto Workers (UAW) contracts in effect until 2019, Ford would not have been able to close the Kentucky plant.[54] Hundreds of people replied to Trump's credit-taking tweet with this counterargument but received no public response.

In early January 2017, just weeks before assuming office, Trump again took credit for relatively small developments in the auto industry. He publicly thanked Ford for "scrapping a new plant in Mexico and creating 700 new jobs in the U.S." but suggested that it was connected to Trump's election win: "This is just the beginning—much more to follow."[55] The next week, Trump connected Ford's development with a similar one at Fiat-Chrysler adding two thousand jobs in Michigan and Ohio, while suggesting that it was due to his tireless work with the opening line: "It's finally happening."[56] In these tweets, Trump positions himself as the prognosticator that knew what was coming and the dealmaker that made it happen. Again, Trump did not make any kind of deal with Ford, who was just giving a "vote of confidence" in the economy,[57] and it is not clear that Trump had any influence on the development with Fiat-Chrysler, which may have been planning this move since 2015.[58] Trump has continued to take credit for jobs developments into the first six months of his presidency, which he may deserve some credit for. Yet these early tweets taking credit, weeks before he was even inaugurated as president, and some of the earliest tweets months before he had become the Republican nominee, are evidence that Trump will take credit wherever he can. Obama has taken credit for similar developments, such as a famous retweet of Joe Biden's statement that "Osama bin Laden is dead, and General Motors is alive" during the reelection campaign in 2012.[59] Yet this claim notably left unsaid that Obama was responsible, and was retweeted four years into Obama's administration, after a historic intervention in General Motors led by Obama's Team Auto.[60] Perhaps more importantly, Trump remained silent on Twitter when the numbers started to go the other way—with Ford reporting cuts of 1,400 jobs, General Motors reporting cuts of 4,400 jobs, and Fiat-Chrysler reporting cuts of 1,300 jobs, according to a June 2017 story by Rein Wilson of *The Hill*.[61] Taking credit and avoiding responsibility have characterized much of Trump's tweets (or lack thereof) on the auto industry to date.

What Trump's tweets on the auto industry have not done is provide much in the way of policy specifics. Beyond the threat of an import border tax, there are few policy details in either Trump's tweets or his speeches. As Paul

A. Eisenstein reported, Trump has met with auto industry leadership twice, "alternately scolded and praised the industry," and has left the industry "still confused." It is not clear to automakers, according to Eisenstein, what Trump plans to do about automation reducing jobs at parts suppliers, how a North American Free Trade Agreement (NAFTA) rework would handle parts that routinely travel over borders, what will happen with infrastructure spending or corporate tax rates, what Trump will ultimately decide to do about the fuel efficiency standards under review, or whether he will take up any of the other regulations the industry wants reconsidered.[62]

This uncertainty seems to come from the lack of details and ambiguity in Trump's public address. Occasional ambiguity has been useful to some former presidents.[63] Yet ambiguity is practically a feature of the 140 character structure of Twitter. Presidents use public address, including social media posts, to signal to constituents about planned policies.[64] Presidential ability to influence national public opinion may be more limited in the social media era, but presidents are still able to target specific groups and use rhetorical appeals to influence those groups. Jeffrey Cohen calls this "Going Local." For businesses in particular, presidential address is a crucial way to gauge the regulatory climate to expect over the next months and years, and how healthy they expect the economy to be.[65] The auto industry is in this situation—looking to Trump for signals and a group that he could conceivably focus on and influence. Trump has provided that local group little of what they are listening for.

The ambiguity leading to uncertainty in these tweets, combined with the threats, individual targeting of companies, and the race to claim credit or avoid responsibility, make Trump's social presence a potentially dangerous development for the institution of the presidency. Next, the chapter concludes with a consideration of how Trump's tweets may shape rhetorical norms for the presidency and contribute to hyper partisanship in American politics.

INFLUENCE ON THE PRESIDENCY AND THE POLITICAL CLIMATE

Donald Trump's tweets may be particularly troubling to rhetoricians. Scholars in presidential rhetoric are familiar with the concept of rhetorical legacies: the idea that presidents, among other kinds of rhetors, do not speak from within a vacuum, but rather are influenced by the weight of presidential address that precedes them. This line of thinking is evident in the presidential speech genre work done by scholars like Karlyn Kohrs Campbell and Kathleen Hall Jamieson.[66] Rhetorical legacies are also a hallmark of the concept of the rhetorical presidency, which has become what it is through the incremental additions by presidents of the post-radio age to the canon of presidential address.[67]

The basic problem with rhetorical legacies and Trump's tweets hinges on whether he continues to tweet in the ways that he has done. If he continues to do so for years, the American public may become accustomed to this new normal. Challengers in 2020 may match blow for blow with Trump on Twitter, who has given no evidence he will cease to use Twitter to attack opponents as he has done since announcing his bid for the presidency. If Trump fills a full term in office, or two, with tweets like those analyzed in this chapter, it will be all the more likely that the next president will follow suit. Idiosyncratic choices, if effective, become the norms of the office, and eventually can become expected of future presidents. There is always the potential for an individual president to break from the norms, as Trump demonstrates, but if those norms are effective, a president is less likely to choose to ignore them. According to White and Woellert, polls show majority approval of Trump directly dealing with companies in public, and Trump's "aggressive approach will be politically popular, leading him to make it a regular feature."[68] Three or four administrations from now, Trump's tweets may be seen as a turning point in the reshaping of "normal" presidential speech.

Furthermore, there is danger that Trump's tweets are contributing to hyper partisanship in American politics. Trump's well-known disdain for the "mainstream media," which has a popular hashtag on Twitter (#MSM), stems from his frequent argument that they do not tell the story the way he wants it told. For example, while president-elect, in a typical tweet about the mainstream media, Trump wrote: "Once again, #MSM is dishonest. 'Schlonged' is not vulgar. When I said Hillary got 'schlonged' that meant beaten badly."[69] Regardless of the definition of "schlong" one chooses to adopt, Trump claims that the mainstream media is dishonest for not using his version of events. Trump supporters see tweets like this one, retweeted 4,100 times, and are provided with evidence that the mainstream media is dishonest. It is not strong evidence. Some might even call it opinion, not evidence. But Trump supporters might see it as evidence, deepening their own distrust of the mainstream media. At the same time, Trump's willingness to publicly write about getting "schlonged" makes him seem *more* honest and genuine to his supporters, deepening their trust in him.

If Trump were correct in calling out media misrepresentations and dishonesty, the developing trust between Trump and some of his supporters would be less concerning. Yet Trump has demonstrated his willingness to repeatedly lie in public addresses. Politifact's file on Donald Trump shows that 69 percent of the over four hundred Trump statements examined by the site were mostly false, false, or a "pants on fire" lie. Fourteen percent were half true, and 17 percent were mostly true or true.[70] Of course, Politifact is part of the mainstream media, so Trump's supporters are already primed to ignore those findings.

Although hypothetical examples can be dangerous, this particular hypothetical is not hard to imagine: Trump claims credit for something he had nothing to do with (such as an automaker adding some jobs at a factory in the Midwest) and then tweets about it. That tweet goes to an audience that is roughly divisible into three categories: those that believe the mainstream media is mostly dishonest, those that believe the mainstream media is mostly honest, and the uninformed or apathetic with no opinion either way. After the tweet taking credit, an institution such as *Politico* publishes an article demonstrating factually why Trump does not deserve credit. The audience that does not trust the mainstream media sees that article as proof of dishonesty. Trump's tweet is its own proof of honesty. Selective exposure begets confirmation bias. The audience that does trust the mainstream media sees the article as proof Trump doesn't deserve credit, and Trump's tweet as proof he is dishonest. Again, selective exposure begets confirmation bias. Yet this all happens on Twitter, a public social media platform where most users can directly address most other users. One side retweets Trump's credit-taking as evidence of his successes and honesty, while the other retweets it with a link to the article as evidence of his boasting and dishonesty. Each side becomes more convinced of the corruption and stupidity of the other, each side becomes less interested in bipartisan conversation. Trump, who can't possibly read twenty thousand replies and retweets, may merely see the level of activity as positive reinforcement and repeat the behavior. The uninformed or apathetic audience with no opinion on the mainstream media sees the vitriol between the two camps and becomes more apathetic, more uninformed, and more disengaged from the political process altogether. The result: more entrenched opposition groups unwilling to consider an alternative perspective and fewer people overall engaged in the political conversation.

Hyper partisanship has been growing in American politics for decades, and Trump's tweets seem likely to make it worse. The mantra of "dishonest media" makes it difficult to counter Trump's "alternative facts" with facts. Trump's aggressive, threatening, and at times abusive manner on Twitter sets the standard by which his followers should engage with what they see as his enemies. Given the way that rhetorical tactics are adopted by successors, Trump's demeanor on Twitter could become the new normal of the American political climate. Americans should resist these changes where possible. Scholars of the presidency, public address, and politics should work harder to provide alternative voices to the masses, rather than just in journal articles behind pay-walls. We need to engage them in public spaces—on Twitter or other social media platforms. A scholar with peer-reviewed articles and published books is not by default part of the "mainstream media" and so may still have some capital in addressing those that no longer trust legacy news networks. We should all take that responsibility seriously.

NOTES

1. Misplaced hyphen in original. Donald J. Trump, Twitter Post. January 3, 2017, 4:30 a.m., https://twitter.com/realDonaldTrump/status/816260343391514624.

2. Vanessa B. Beasley, *You, the People: American National Identity in Presidential Rhetoric* (College Station: Texas A&M University Press, 2004); Mary E. Stuckey, *Defining Americans: The Presidency and National Identity* (Lawrence: University Press of Kansas, 2004); David Zarefsky, "Presidential Rhetoric and the Power of Definition," *Presidential Studies Quarterly* 34.3 (2004); Kathryn M. Olson, "The Controversy over President Reagan's Visit to Bitburg: Strategies of Definition and Redefinition," *Quarterly Journal of Speech* 75.2 (1989); Samuel Kernell, *Going Public: New Strategies of Presidential Leadership*, 3 ed. (Washington DC: CQ Press, 1997); Jeffrey E. Cohen, "Presidential Rhetoric and the Public Agenda," *American Journal of Political Science* 39.1 (1995); Bernard C. Cohen, *The Press and Foreign Policy* (Princeton: Princeton University Press, 1963); Meena Bose, "Words as Signals: Drafting Cold War Rhetoric in the Eisenhower and Kennedy Administrations," *Congress & the Presidency* 25.1 (1998); Matthew Eshbaugh-Soha, *The President's Speeches: Beyond Going Public* (Boulder, CO: Lynne Rienner Press, 2006).

3. Frank Schnell and Karen Callaghan, "Terrorism, Media Frames, and Framing Effects: A Macro- and Microlevel Analysis," *Framing American Politics*, eds. Karen Callaghan and Frank Schnell (Pittsburg: University of Pittsburgh Press, 2005); David M. Rankin, "Featuring the President as Free Trader: Television News Coverage of U.S. Trade Policies," *Presidential Studies Quarterly* 36.4 (2006); Kim L. Fridkin and Patrick J. Kenney, "Campaign Frames: Can Candidates Influence Media Coverage?," *Framing American Politics*, eds. Karen Callaghan and Frank Schnell (Pittsburg: University of Pittsburgh Press, 2005).

4. Teena Gabrielson, "Obstacles and Opportunities: Factors That Constrain Elected Officials' Ability to Frame Political Issues," *Framing American Politics*, eds. Karen Callaghan and Frank Schnell (Pittsburg: University of Pittsburgh Press, 2005); Brandon Rottinghaus, *The Provisional Pulpit: Modern Presidential Leadership of Public Opinion* (College Station: Texas A&M University Press, 2010); Matthew Corrigan, "The Transformation of Going Public: President Clinton, the First Lady, and Health Care Reform," *Political Communication* 17 (2000); George C. Edwards III, *On Deaf Ears: The Limits of the Bully Pulpit* (New Haven: Yale University Press, 2003).

5. Kendra Marr, "Toyota Passes GM as World's Largest Automaker," 2009, *Washington Post*, http://www.washingtonpost.com/wp-dyn/content/article/2009/01/21/AR2009012101216.html, 6–15–2017.

6. *Fortune*, "Fortune 500: Biggest Employers, 2017," *Fortune/Time*, http://fortune.com/fortune500/list/filtered?sortBy=employees&first500, 8–28–2017.

7. BLS, "Automotive Industry: Employment, Earnings, and Hours," 2017, Bureau of Labor Statistics—United States Department of Labor, https://www.bls.gov/iag/tgs/iagauto.htm, 8/1/2017.

8. "When one of [GM's] top executives, Charlie 'Engine' Wilson, left GM to become Eisenhower's defense secretary, he was widely quoted as saying that what was good for General Motors was good for the country" (118). David Halberstam, *The Fifties* (New York: Fawcett Columbine, 1993).

9. For more on presidential speech about auto industry issues over the last four decades, see: Steve A. Stuglin, "'Let Detroit Go Bankrupt:' Using the Past to Win the Present," *The 2012 Presidential Election: A Transformation in National Politics*, eds. Douglas M. Brattebo, Tom Lansford, and Jack Covarrubias (Akron, OH: University of Akron Press, 2014) Steve A. Stuglin, "U.S. Auto Industry Rescue," *The Obama Presidency: A Preliminary Assessment*, eds. Robert P. Watson, Jack Covarrubias, Tom Lansford, and Douglas M. Brattebo (New York: SUNY, 2012).

10. Richard M. Nixon, Remarks at a Question and Answer Session at a Ten Member Panel of the Economic Club of Detroit, 9/23/71, Woolley & Peters, Santa Barbara, CA, 1971.

11. Jody Powell, "Signing Ceremony for H.R. 5860, the Chrysler Loan (the Cabinet Room)," Staff Offices—Office of the Chief of Staff—Butler Box 139 "UAW 9/21/78–9/12/80" (Atlanta, GA: Carter Presidential Library, 1979), vol, Barack H. Obama, "Statement by the Preisdent-Elect on the Auto Industry Assistance Package," 12/19/2008, Woolley & Peters, Santa Barbara, CA, 2008; George W. Bush, "Remarks on the American Auto Industry," 12/19/2008, Woolley & Peters, Santa Barbara, CA, 2008.

12. Donald J. Trump, "Remarks at a Meeting of the President's Strategic and Policy Forum," 2/3/2017, Woolley & Peters, Santa Barbara, CA, 2017; Donald J. Trump, "Remarks at a Roundtable Discussion with Aviation Industry Representatives," 2/9/2017, Woolley & Peters, Santa Barbara, CA, 2017; Donald J. Trump, "The President's News Conference with Prime Minister Shinzo Abe of Japan," 2/10/2017, Woolley & Peters, Santa Barbara, CA, 2017; Donald J. Trump, "The President's News Conference with Prime Minister Justin P. J. Trudeau of Canada," 2/13/2017.

Woolley & Peters, Santa Barbara, CA, 2017; Donald J. Trump, "The President's News Conference," 2/16/2017, Woolley & Peters, Santa Barbara, CA, 2017; Donald J. Trump, "Remarks at the Boeing Company Manufacturing Facility in North Charleston, South Carolina," 2/17/2017, Woolley & Peters, Santa Barbara, CA, 2017; Donald. J. Trump, Remarks at a Listening Session with Manufacturing Industry Leaders, 2/23/2017, Woolley & Peters, Santa Barbara, CA, 2017; Donald J. Trump, "Remarks at the Conservative Political Action Conference in National Harbor, Maryland," 2/24/2017, Woolley & Peters, Santa Barbara, CA, 2017.

13. Nixon, "Remarks at a Question and Answer Session at a Ten Member Panel of the Economic Club of Detroit," 9/23/71.

14. Ronald W. Reagan, Statement on Assistance for the Domestic Automobile Industry, 4/6/1981, Woolley & Peters, http://www.presidency.ucsb.edu/ws/index.php?pid=43655.

15. Donald J. Trump, "Remarks at the American Center for Mobility in Ypsilanti Township, Michigan," 3/15/2017, Woolley & Peters, Santa Barbara, CA, 2017.

16. See, for example: Donald J. Trump, "The President's Weekly Address," 3/18/2017, Woolley & Peters, Santa Barbara, CA, 2017; Trump, "Remarks at a Roundtable Discussion with Aviation Industry Representatives," 2/9/2017, Trump, "The President's News Conference with Prime Minister Justin P. J. Trudeau of Canada," 2/13/2017.

17. Obama blamed the industry for resisting regulations, failing to respond to global changes, making poor decisions, and assuming unsustainable amounts of debt. See: Barack H. Obama, "Remarks on Fuel Efficiency Standards," 5/19/2009, Woolley & Peters, Santa Barbara, CA, 2009; Barack H. Obama, "Remarks on the United States Automobile Industry," 6/1/2009, Woolley & Peters, Santa Barbara, CA, 2009.

18. Jimmy Carter, "Untitled—Delivery Copy for Speech on 7/8/80 [and Attached Handwritten Notes]," Staff Offices—Office of the Secretary of State, Presidential Handwriting File Box 194, "Trip to California, Florida, Georgia, Detroit, Alaska, and Japan 7/3/80–7/17/80" (Atlanta, GA: Carter Presidential Library, 1980), vol, James E. Carter, Detroit, MI: "Remarks to Reporters Following a Meeting with Automobile Industry Representatives," rec 7/8/1980, Woolley & Peters, Santa Barbara, CA, 1980.

19. Roland Evans and Robert Novak, *The Reagan Revolution* (New York: E. P. Dutton, 1981), 153–154; Lou Cannon, *Reagan* (New York: G.P. Putnam's Sons, 1982), 324.

20. Donald J. Trump, "Interview with Bill O'Reilly of Fox News," 2/3/2017, Woolley & Peters, Santa Barbara, CA, 2017; Trump, "Remarks at a Listening Session with Manufacturing Industry Leaders," 2/23/2017; Trump, "Remarks at the American Center for Mobility in Ypsilanti Township, Michigan," 3/15/2017.

21. Michael L. Bromley, *William Howard Taft and the First Motoring Presidency, 1909–1913* (Jefferson, NC: McFarland & Co., 2003).

22. John F. Kennedy, "Speech of Senator John F. Kennedy, Detroit Coliseum, Michigan State Fair, Detroit, MI," 10/26/1960, Woolley & Peters, Santa Barbara, CA, 1960; James E. Carter, Wayne, MI "Remarks to Employees of the Ford Auto Assembly Plant" 10/1/80, Woolley & Peters, Santa Barbara, CA, 1980; George H. W. Bush, "Remarks to the Economic Club of Detroit in Detroit, Michigan," 3/13/92, Woolley & Peters, Santa Barbara, CA, 1992; Barack H. Obama, "Remarks to the Detroit Economic Club," 5/7/2007, Woolley & Peters, http://www.presidency.ucsb.edu/ws/index.php?pid=77000.

23. Trump, "Remarks at the American Center for Mobility in Ypsilanti Township, Michigan," 3/15/2017.

24. Trump, "Remarks at the American Center for Mobility in Ypsilanti Township, Michigan, 3/15/2017.

25. David Shepardson, "Trump Suggests Moving Some Car Production from Michigan," 2015, *Detroit News*, http://www.detroitnews.com/story/news/politics/2015/04/17/rubio-criticizes-billion-auto-bailout/25950819/, 8/15/2016.

26. Gina Masullo Chen, "Tweet This: A Uses and Gratifications Perspective on How Active Twitter Use Gratifies a Need to Connect with Others," *Computers in Human Behavior* 27 (2011).

27. Janet Johnson, "Twitter Bites and Romney: Examining the Rhetorical Situation of the 2012 Presidential Election in 140 Characters," *Journal of Contemporary Rhetoric* 2.3 (2012), 63.

28. Benjamin Mullin, "Report: Journalists Are Largest, Most Active Verified Group on Twitter," 2015, Poynter, https://www.poynter.org/2015/report-journalists-are-largest-most-active-group-on-twitter/346957/, (January 1, 2016).

29. Brett Molina, "Twitter Says Politics Is Bringing Back Some Users," 2017, *USA Today*, https://www.usatoday.com/story/tech/news/2017/04/26/twitter-shares-jump-after-beating-estimates/100921470/, (July 10, 2017).

30. Andranik Tumasjan, Tim O. Sprenger, Phillip G. Sandner, and Isabell M. Welpe, "Election Forecasts with Twitter: How 140 Characters Reflect the Political Landscape," *Social Science Computer Review* 29.4 (2010).

31. Kyle Leighton and David Taintor, "Hashtages Are the New Lawn Signs: Why Twitter Won't Predict Political Success in the 2012 Cycle," 2012, http://www.niemanlab.org/2012/03/hashtags-are-the-new-lawn-signs-why-twitter-wont-predict-political-success-in-the-2012-cycle/, (June 1, 2017).

32. Erica J. Seifert, *The Politics of Authenticity in Presidential Campaigns, 1976–2008* (Jefferson, NC: Macfarland, 2012).

33. Gary C. Woodward, *Center Stage: Media and the Performance of American Politics* (New York: Rowman & Littlefield Publishers, 2007), 100.

34. Nisha Chittal, "George W. Bush and Bill Clinton Swap Snark on Social Media," 2014, MSNBC, http://www.msnbc.com/msnbc/george-w-bush-and-bill-clinton-swap-snark-social-media, (July 20, 2017).

35. Glenn Thrush and Maggie Haberman, "Trump Mocks Mika Brzezinski; Says She Was 'Bleeding Badly from a Face-Lift,'" 2017, *New York Times*, https://www.nytimes.com/2017/06/29/business/media/trump-mika-brzezinski-facelift.html, (June 29, 2017).

36. Johnson, "Twitter Bites and Romney: Examining the Rhetorical Situation of the 2012 Presidential Election in 140 Characters."

37. Annelise Russell, "U.S. Senators on Twitter: Asymmetric Party Rhetoric in 140 Characters," *American Politics Research* (2017).

38. Ramona Kreis, "The 'Tweet Politics' of President Trump," J*ournal of Language and Politics* (2017); Jack Holland and Ben Fermor, "Trump's Rhetoric at 100 Days: Contradictions within Effective Emotional Narratives," *Critical Studies on Security* (2017).

39. Brian L. Ott, "The Age of Twitter: Donald J. Trump and the Politics of Debasement," *Critical Studies in Media Communication* 34.1 (2016).

40. Neil Savage, "Twitter as Medium and Message," *Communications of the Association for Computing Machinery* 54.3 (2011).

41. Friend or Follow, Twitter: Most Followed, 2017, Floating Head Studios, http://friendorfollow.com/twitter/most-followers/, (September 30, 2017).

42. According to the database of speeches held by the American Presidency Project. Gerhard Peters and John T. Woolley, The American Presidency Project, 2009, http://www.presidency.ucsb.edu/.

43. Donald J. Trump, Twitter Post, January 5, 2017, 10:14 a.m., https://twitter.com/realDonaldTrump/status/817071792711942145.

44. Trump, Twitter Post, January 3, 2017, 4:30 a.m., https://twitter.com/realDonaldTrump/status/816260343391514624.

45. Donald J. Trump, Twitter Post, July 14, 2015, 5:55 a.m., https://twitter.com/realDonaldTrump/status/620939800888127488.

46. Ben White and Lorraine Woellert, "Trump's Tweet Shaming Startles Corporate America," 2016, *Politico*, http://www.politico.com/story/2016/12/trumps-tweet-shaming-corporate-america-232274, (February 2, 2017).

47. Donald J. Trump and Tony Schwartz, *Trump: The Art of the Deal* (New York: Random House, 1992).

48. Trump and Schwartz, *Trump: The Art of the Deal*.

49. Kate Kelly, Rachel Abrams, and Alan Rappeport, "Trump Is Said to Abandon Contentious Border Tax on Imports," 2017, *New York Times*, https://www.nytimes.com/2017/04/25/us/politics/orrin-hatch-trump-tax-cuts-deficit-economy.html, (August 1, 2017).

50. Donald J. Trump, Twitter Post, October 25, 2015, 3:36 p.m., https://twitter.com/realDonaldTrump/status/658381595049611265.

51. "Do you think I will get credit for keeping Ford in U.S. Who cares, my supporters know the truth. Think what can be done as president!" Donald J. Trump, Twitter Post, October 25, 2015, 1:39 p.m., https://twitter.com/realDonaldTrump/status/658382301324251136.

52. Spelling error present in original. Donald J. Trump, Twitter Post, November 17, 2016, 9:01 p.m., https://twitter.com/realDonaldTrump/status/799432403727028224.

53. Donald J. Trump, Twitter Post, November 17, 2016, 9:15 p.m., https://twitter.com/realDonaldTrump/status/799435824622252032.

54. Louis Nelson, "Trump Takes Credit for Keeping Ford Plant in U.S. That Wasn't Leaving," 2016, *Politico*, http://www.politico.com/story/2016/11/trump-ford-plant-tweet-231597, (February 1, 2017).

55. Donald J. Trump, Twitter Post, January 4, 2017, 8:19 a.m., https://twitter.com/realDonaldTrump/status/816635078067490816.

56. Donald J. Trump, Twitter Post, January 9, 2017, 6:14 a.m., https://twitter.com/realDonaldTrump/status/818460862675558400; Donald J. Trump, Twitter Post, January 9, 2017, 6:16 a.m., https://twitter.com/realDonaldTrump/status/818461467766824961.

57. Louis Nelson, "Trump Thanks Ford for Halting Mexico Plant," 2017, *Politico*, http://www.politico.com/story/2017/01/trump-thanks-ford-motor-company-233172, (March 1, 2017).

58. Louis Nelson, "Trump Commends Fiat Chrysler for Investing in U.S. Plants," 2017, *Politico*, http://www.politico.com/story/2017/01/trump-praise-fiat-chrysler-233346, (March 5, 2017).

59. Barack Obama, Twitter Post, September 6, 2012, 6:56 p.m., https://twitter.com/BarackObama/status/243890464149868544.

60. Steven Rattner, *Overhaul: Insider's Account of the Obama Administration's Emergency Rescue of the Auto Industry* (Boston: Houghton Mifflin Harcourt, 2010).

61. Rein Wilson, "Trump's Job Promises Face Challenge in Auto Sector," 2017, *The Hill*, http://thehill.com/homenews/state-watch/339055-trumps-job-promises-face-challenge-in-auto-sector, (July 10, 2017).

62. Paul Eisenstein, "After 100 Days, Auto Industry Still Confused about Where Trump Is Heading," 2017, *NBC News*, http://www.nbcnews.com/storyline/president-trumps-first-100-days/after-100-days-auto-industry-still-confused-about-where-trump-n752476, (May 5, 2017).

63. Mary E. Stuckey, *Jimmy Carter, Human Rights, and the National Agenda* (College Station: Texas A&M University Press, 2008), 131.

64. Bose, "Words as Signals: Drafting Cold War Rhetoric in the Eisenhower and Kennedy Administrations."

65. B. Dan Wood, "Presidential Rhetoric and Economic Leadership," *Presidential Studies Quarterly* 34.3 (2004).

66. Karlyn Kohrs Campbell and Kathleen Hall Jamieson, *Presidents Creating the Presidency: Deeds Done in Words* (Chicago: University of Chicago Press, 2008).

67. Jeffrey Tulis, *The Rhetorical Presidency* (Princeton, NJ: Priceton University Press, 1987); Jeffrey Tulis, "Revising the Rhetorical Presidency," *Beyond the Rhetorical Presidency*, ed. Martin J. Medhurst (College Station: Texas A&M University Press, 1996); Mary E. Stuckey, "Rethinking the Rhetorical Presidency and Presidential Rhetoric," *Review of Communication* 10.1 (2010).

68. White and Woellert, "Trump's Tweet Shaming Startles Corporate America."

69. Donald J. Trump, Twitter Post, December 22, 2015, 4:47 p.m., https://twitter.com/realDonaldTrump/status/679463426675097600.

70. Politifact, "Donald Trump's File," 2017, Politifact's Truth-O-Meter, Available: http://www.politifact.com/personalities/donald-trump/, (August 2, 2017).

Index

About the Editor

Regina Luttrell, PhD, is assistant professor of social media and public relations at the S. I. Newhouse School of Public Communications at Syracuse University. She spent the first half of her career managing high-level public relations and marketing activities for Fortune 500 companies, governmental entities, and non-profit organizations. Upon leaving corporate America she earned her PhD to teach public relations and social media at the University level. A contributor to *PR Tactics*, *PR News*, book chapters, as well as peer-reviewed journals, she is a noted speaker frequently presenting at national and international conferences and business events on topics related to the current social media revolution, the ongoing public relations evolution, and Millennials within the classroom and workplace. She is the (co)author of multiple books, including: *Social Media: How to Engage, Share, and Connect*; *The Millennial Mindset: Unraveling Fact from Fiction*; *Brew Your Business: The Ultimate Craft Beer Playbook*; *Public Relations Campaigns: An Integrated Approach*; *The PR Agency Handbook*; and *A Practical Guide to Ethics in Public Relations*.

About the Contributors

Robert J. Baron, PhD, is an assistant professor at Austin Peay State University where he is a digital media researcher and professor. He taught as a graduate instructor in both the Communication Studies and Writing Studies departments at the University of Minnesota–Twin Cities. Baron describes his educational and research interests as internet studies, gaming studies, rhetorical theory, and technical and professional communication.

Dwight DeWerth-Pallmeyer is an associate professor of communication studies and of digital media informatics at Widener University. He is the author of the book, *The Audience In the News*, producer of the feature documentary, *The Critics: Stories from the Inside Pages* (Films Media Group), and producer of the 2018 documentary, *Cellular Aftershocks*. He chaired the Communication Studies program at Widener University from 1999 to 2014, and has also taught in the journalism program at Cal Poly San Luis Obispo, CA, and the Speech Communications programs at Utica College, Utica, New York, and Augustana College, Rock Island, Illinois. He also served as a radio news director in both Illinois and Wyoming and has reported extensively for National Public Radio, Monitor Radio, and CBS radio networks. He holds a PhD in communication studies from Northwestern University, an MA in mass communication from the University of Minnesota, and a BA in journalism from Valparaiso University. He is frequently cited in publications such as *USA Today*, *Forbes*, the *Christian Science Monitor*, *Parade Magazine*, the *Philadelphia Inquirer*, the *Baltimore Sun*, *WebMD* and *FoxNews.com*.

Arvind Diddi, PhD is an associate professor of journalism and mass communication in the Department of Communication Studies at the State University of New York at Oswego. Dr. Diddi teaches introductory and advanced news writing and reporting courses in addition to the history of American journalism, and mass media research methods. Dr. Diddi's research areas are news media bias, news media framing, media sociology, and news media use. He has about ten publications in peer-reviewed mass communication journals such as the *Journal of Broadcasting & Electronic Media, Mass Communication & Society*, and has nearly twenty conference papers. Dr. Diddi earned his doctoral degree in mass media from Michigan State University, and before that he worked as a reporter for six years.

Paige L. Gibson, a recent DAAD grant recipient, is a PhD candidate in media and communication at Temple University. She is interested in the intersection of social memory, communication technologies, and cultural identity. She has published in ESSACHESS and the Palgrave Macmillan Memory Studies series, Memory in a Mediated World.

Jennifer Grygiel is an assistant professor at the S. I. Newhouse School of Public Communications at Syracuse University. Grygiel teaches courses in social media and a class in collaboration with BuzzFeed. In 2016, Grygiel took first place in the Best Practices in Ethics in an Emerging Media Environment teaching competition, sponsored by the Association for Education in Journalism and Mass Communication (AEJMC) Elected Committee on Teaching. Grygiel conducts research in the areas of social media; emerging media; corporate social responsibility; financial technology ("Fintech"); trust and safety; platform governance; e-government; community policing; LGBTQ youth advocacy; social justice and race, gender and society. Grygiel is a social media professional who most recently served as social business and emerging media manager at a global financial institution where they developed a social listening and marketing data and analytics program. They also served as the lead project manager there for the Social Intranet Project, which received an IABC Gold Quill Merit Award. Grygiel's social listening work was also recognized and received a Gold Wommy for Social Media Monitoring Implementation from Womma (Word of Mouth Marketing Association). She earned a bachelor's in art and education from St. Lawrence University and completed the graduate program in management (ALM) with a concentration in finance and control from Harvard Extension School.

Stephanie Madden, PhD, is an assistant professor in the Department of Journalism and Strategic Media at the University of Memphis. Her research explores the intersection between public relations, activism, risk/crisis communication, and social media. She earned her PhD from the University of Maryland. Previously, Dr. Madden was a full-time communication researcher at the National Consortium for the Study of Terrorism and Responses to Terrorism (START), a Department of Homeland Security Center of Excellence. Recent publications appear in the *Journal of Contingencies and Crisis Management*, *Communication Teacher*, *Public Relations Review*, and *Review of Communication*.

Brian Moritz, PhD, is an assistant professor of digital media production and online journalism at SUNY Oswego. His research revolves around the social construction of news and media sociology. He is a former newspaper sports reporter and columnist, and earned graduate degrees from Syracuse University.

Michael J. Steudeman, PhD, is a visiting assistant professor in the Department of Communication at the University of Memphis. His research explores presidential rhetoric, education policy, and argumentation theory. He earned his PhD from the University of Maryland. Previously, he has worked as a research assistant for The Century Foundation and spent two years with Teach for America. His work appears in the *Quarterly Journal of Speech*, *Rhetoric & Public Affairs*, and *Communication Quarterly*.

Leysan Khakimova Storie, PhD, is an assistant professor in the College of Communication and Media Sciences at Zayed University in the United Arab Emirates. Prior to getting her PhD from the University of Maryland, Dr. Storie was a Fulbright scholar at the University of Kansas. She has experience working in international organizations, including the United Nations, and in tourism. Her research focuses on global public relations and public diplomacy, and has been published in the *International Journal of Strategic Communication*, *Public Relations Review*, and *Journal of Intercultural Communication Research*.

Steve A. Stuglin, PhD is an award-winning teacher and assistant professor of communication at Georgia Highlands College. His research interests include political rhetoric and public policy, with a focus on the relationships between storied institutions. He has written extensively on the relationship between the domestic auto industry and the presidency and presented this work in two dozen conference presentations, including at meetings of the National Communication Association, the Southern States Communication Association, and the Rhetoric Society of America. His forthcoming work “Obligations to Act: The Rhetorical Legacy of the Rescues of the Domestic Auto Industry” will appear in *The Legacy of the Obama Presidency* (TAMU). His work has also been published in *The Presidential Election of 2012: A Transformation in American National Politics* and *The Obama Presidency: A Preliminary Assessment*.

Chiaoning Su, PhD is an assistant professor of communication and journalism at Oakland University. Her research explores the political and cultural roles of journalism in times of disaster in a global and specifically Asian context. She has published in journals such as *Media, Culture and Society*, *Asian Journal of Communication*, *Asian Cinema*, *China Media Research* and in the Palgrave Macmillan Memory Studies series, *Memory in a Mediated World*.